Practice*Pla*

Arthur E. Jongsr

Helping therapists help their cl...

Treatment Planners cover all the necessary elements for developing formal treatment plans, including detailed problem definitions, long-term goals, short-term objectives, therapeutic interventions, and DSM-IV™ diagnoses.

- ❏ The Complete Adult Psychotherapy Treatment Planner, Fourth Edition...........0-471-76346-2 / $49.95
- ❏ The Child Psychotherapy Treatment Planner, Fourth Edition ....0-471-78535-0 / $49.95
- ❏ The Adolescent Psychotherapy Treatment Planner, Fourth Edition ....0-471-78539-3 / $49.95
- ❏ The Addiction Treatment Planner, Third Edition...0-471-72544-7 / $49.95
- ❏ The Couples Psychotherapy Treatment Planner ....0-471-24711-1 / $49.95
- ❏ The Group Therapy Treatment Planner, Second Edition..................................0-471-66791-9 / $49.95
- ❏ The Family Therapy Treatment Planner ....0-471-34768-X / $49.95
- ❏ The Older Adult Psychotherapy Treatment Planner ....0-471-29574-4 / $49.95
- ❏ The Employee Assistance (EAP) Treatment Planner ....0-471-24709-X / $49.95
- ❏ The Gay and Lesbian Psychotherapy Treatment Planner ....0-471-35080-X / $49.95
- ❏ The Crisis Counseling and Traumatic Events Treatment Planner ....0-471-39587-0 / $49.95
- ❏ The Social Work and Human Services Treatment Planner ....0-471-37741-4 / $49.95
- ❏ The Continuum of Care Treatment Planner ....0-471-19568-5 / $49.95
- ❏ The Behavioral Medicine Treatment Planner..0-471-31923-6 / $49.95
- ❏ The Mental Retardation and Developmental Disability Treatment Planner ....0-471-38253-1 / $49.95
- ❏ The Special Education Treatment Planner...0-471-38872-6 / $49.95
- ❏ The Severe and Persistent Mental Illness Treatment Planner......................0-471-35945-9 / $49.95
- ❏ The Personality Disorders Treatment Planner ....0-471-39403-3 / $49.95
- ❏ The Rehabilitation Psychology Treatment Planner ....0-471-35178-4 / $49.95
- ❏ The Pastoral Counseling Treatment Planner...0-471-25416-9 / $49.95
- ❏ The Juvenile Justice and Residential Care Treatment Planner ....0-471-43320-9 / $49.95
- ❏ The School Counseling and School Social Work Treatment Planner ....0-471-08496-4 / $49.95
- ❏ The Psychopharmacology Treatment Planner ....0-471-43322-5 / $49.95
- ❏ The Probation and Parole Treatment Planner..0-471-20244-4 / $49.95
- ❏ The Suicide and Homicide Risk Assessment
  and Prevention Treatment Planner ....0-471-46631-X / $49.95
- ❏ The Speech-Language Pathology Treatment Planner.....................................0-471-27504-2 / $49.95
- ❏ The College Student Counseling Treatment Planner ....0-471-46708-1 / $49.95
- ❏ The Parenting Skills Treatment Planner ....0-471-48183-1 / $49.95
- ❏ The Early Childhood Education Intervention Treatment Planner ....0-471-65962-2 / $49.95
- ❏ The Co-Occurring Disorders Treatment Planner..0-471-73081-5 / $49.95

The **Complete Treatment and Homework Planners** series of books combines our bestselling *Treatment Planners* and *Homework Planners* into one easy-to-use, all-in-one resource for mental health professionals treating clients suffering from the most commonly diagnosed disorders.

- ❏ The Complete Depression Treatment and Homework Planner......................0-471-64515-X / $39.95
- ❏ The Complete Anxiety Treatment and Homework Planner ....0-471-64548-6 / $39.95

Practice*Planners*®

Homework Planners feature dozens of behaviorally based, ready-to-use assignments that are designed for use between sessions, as well as a disk (Microsoft Word) containing all of the assignments—allowing you to customize them to suit your unique client needs.

❑ Brief Therapy Homework Planner...0-471-24611-5 / $49.95
❑ Brief Couples Therapy Homework Planner..0-471-29511-6 / $49.95
❑ Child Therapy Homework Planner, Second Edition.......................................0-471-78534-2 / $49.95
❑ Child Therapy Activity and Homework Planner ....0-471-25684-6 / $49.95
❑ Adolescent Therapy Homework Planner, Second Edition..............................0-471-78537-7 / $49.95
❑ Addiction Treatment Homework Planner, Second Edition.............................0-471-27459-3 / $49.95
❑ Brief Employee Assistance Homework Planner..0-471-38088-1 / $49.95
❑ Brief Family Therapy Homework Planner...0-471-38512-3 / $49.95
❑ Grief Counseling Homework Planner...0-471-43318-7 / $49.95
❑ Divorce Counseling Homework Planner ....0-471-43319-5 / $49.95
❑ Group Therapy Homework Planner...0-471-41822-6 / $49.95
❑ School Counseling and School Social Work Homework Planner...................0-471-09114-6 / $49.95
❑ Adolescent Psychotherapy Homework Planner II..0-471-27493-3 / $49.95
❑ Adult Psychotherapy Homework Planner, Second Edition............................0-471-76343-8 / $49.95
❑ Parenting Skills Homework Planner...0-471-48182-3 / $49.95

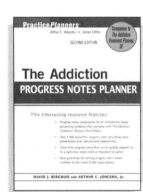

Progress Notes Planners contain complete prewritten progress notes for each presenting problem in the companion Treatment Planners.

❑ The Adult Psychotherapy Progress Notes Planner ....0-471-76344-6 / $49.95
❑ The Adolescent Psychotherapy Progress Notes Planner...............................0-471-78538-5 / $49.95
❑ The Severe and Persistent Mental Illness Progress Notes Planner ....0-471-21986-X / $49.95
❑ The Child Psychotherapy Progress Notes Planner ....0-471-78536-9 / $49.95
❑ The Addiction Progress Notes Planner ....0-471-73253-2 / $49.95
❑ The Couples Psychotherapy Progress Notes Planner....................................0-471-27460-7 / $49.95
❑ The Family Therapy Progress Notes Planner...0-471-48443-1 / $49.95

Client Education Handout Planners contain elegantly designed handouts that can be printed out from the enclosed CD-ROM and provide information on a wide range of psychological and emotional disorders and life skills issues. Use as patient literature, handouts at presentations, and aids for promoting your mental health practice.

❑ Adult Client Education Handout Planner..0-471-20232-0 / $49.95
❑ Child and Adolescent Client Education Handout Planner ....0-471-20233-9 / $49.95
❑ Couples and Family Client Education Handout Planner ....0-471-20234-7 / $49.95

Name _____
Affiliation_____
Address _____
City/State/Zip_____
Phone/Fax_____
E-mail_____
❑ Check enclosed   ❑ Visa   ❑ MasterCard   ❑ American Express
Card # _____
Expiration Date _____
Signature _____
*Add $5 shipping for first book, $3 for each additional book. Please add your local sales tax to all orders.
Prices subject to change without notice.*

■ **To order by phone in the US:**
Call toll free 1-877-762-2974

■ **Online: www.practiceplanners.wiley.com**

■ **Mail this order form to:**
John Wiley & Sons, Attn: J. Knott,
111 River Street, Hoboken, NJ 07030

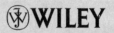

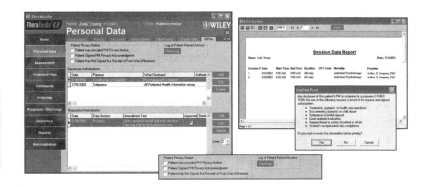

Need Help Getting Started?

Getting Started in Personal and Executive Coaching offers a go-to reference designed to help build, manage, and sustain a thriving coaching practice. Packed with hundreds of proven strategies and techniques, this nuts-and-bolts guide covers all aspects of the coaching business with step-by-step instructions and real-world illustrations that prepare you for every phase of starting your own coaching business.

This single, reliable book offers straightforward advice and tools for running a successful practice, including:

- Seven secrets of highly successful coaches
- Fifteen strategies for landing paying clients
- Ten marketing mistakes to avoid
- Sample business and marketing plans
- Worksheets for setting rates and managing revenue

Getting Started in Personal and Executive Coaching
Stephen G. Fairley and Chris E. Stout
ISBN 0-471-42624-5
Paper • $24.95 • 356pp • December 2003

Getting Started in Private Practice provides all the information you need to confidently start and grow your own mental health practice. This book breaks down the ingredients of practice into more manageable and achievable components and will teach you the skills you need to avoid making costly mistakes. Containing dozens of tools that you can use to achieve your goals, this book has specific information that can be applied to your business today, worksheets that will help you calculate the true costs of various expenditures and activities, checklists that might save you from disaster, and lists of resources to investigate. Includes:

- Forms and examples of various practice aspects
- Step-by-step advice on writing a business plan and marketing your business
- Suggestions and ideas intended to help you get your creative juices flowing
- Practical and simple formulas to help calculate rates, revenues, and Return on Investment
- Comprehensive information on licensing procedures and risk management

Getting Started in Private Practice
Chris E. Stout and Laurie Cope Grand
ISBN 0-471-42623-7
Paper • $24.95 • 304 pp. • October 2004

WILEY

Now you know.

wiley.com

The Speech-Language Pathology Treatment Planner

Practice*Planners*® Series

Treatment Planners

The Complete Adult Psychotherapy Treatment Planner, Third Edition
The Child Psychotherapy Treatment Planner, Third Edition
The Adolescent Psychotherapy Treatment Planner, Third Edition
The Addiction Treatment Planner, Second Edition
The Continuum of Care Treatment Planner
The Couples Psychotherapy Treatment Planner
The Employee Assistance Treatment Planner
The Pastoral Counseling Treatment Planner
The Older Adult Psychotherapy Treatment Planner
The Behavioral Medicine Treatment Planner
The Group Therapy Treatment Planner
The Gay and Lesbian Psychotherapy Treatment Planner
The Family Therapy Treatment Planner
The Severe and Persistent Mental Illness Treatment Planner
The Mental Retardation and Developmental Disability Treatment Planner
The Social Work and Human Services Treatment Planner
The Crisis Counseling and Traumatic Events Treatment Planner
The Personality Disorders Treatment Planner
The Rehabilitation Psychology Treatment Planner
The Special Education Treatment Planner
The Juvenile Justice and Residential Care Treatment Planner
The School Counseling and School Social Work Treatment Planner
The Sexual Abuse Victim and Sexual Offender Treatment Planner
The Probation and Parole Treatment Planner
The Psychopharmacology Treatment Planner
The Speech-Language Pathology Treatment Planner
The Suicide and Homicide Risk Assessment & Prevention Treatment Planner
The College Student Counseling Treatment Planner

Progress Note Planners

The Child Psychotherapy Progress Notes Planner, Second Edition
The Adolescent Psychotherapy progress Notes Planner, Second Edition
The Adult Psychotherapy Progress Notes Planner, Second Edition
The Addiction Progress Notes Planner
The Severe and Persistent Mental Illness Progress Notes Planner
The Couples Psychotherapy Progress Notes Planner

Homework Planners

Brief Therapy Homework Planner
Brief Couples Therapy Homework Planner
Brief Adolescent Therapy Homework Planner
Brief Child Therapy Homework Planner
Brief Employee Assistance Homework Planner
Brief Family Therapy Homework Planner
Grief Counseling Homework Planner
Group Therapy Homework Planner
Divorce Counseling Homework Planner
School Counseling and School Social Work Homework Planner
Child Therapy Activity and Homework Planner
Addiction Treatment Homework Planner, Second Edition
Adolescent Psychotherapy Homework Planner II
Adult Psychotherapy Homework Planner

Client Education Handout Planners

Adult Client Education Handout Planner
Child and Adolescent Client Education Handout Planner
Couples and Family Client Education Handout Planner

Documentation Sourcebooks

The Clinical Documentation Sourcebook, Second Edition
The Forensic Documentation Sourcebook
The Psychotherapy Documentation Primer
The Chemical Dependence Treatment Documentation Sourcebook
The Clinical Child Documentation Sourcebook
The Couple and Family Clinical Documentation Sourcebook
The Continuum of Care Clinical Documentation Sourcebook

Complete Planners

The Complete Depression Treatment and Homework Planner
The Complete Anxiety Treatment and Homework Planner

Practice*Planners*®

Arthur E. Jongsma, Jr., Series Editor

The Speech-Language Pathology Treatment Planner

Keith Landis

Judith Vander Woude

Arthur E. Jongsma, Jr.

WILEY

JOHN WILEY & SONS, INC.

Published by John Wiley & Sons, Inc., Hoboken, New Jersey.
Published simultaneously in Canada.

For general information on our other products and services please contact our Customer Care Department within the United States at (800) 762-2974, outside the United States at (317) 572-3993 or fax (317) 572-4002.

Wiley also publishes its books in a variety of electronic formats. Some content that appears in print may not be available in electronic books. For more information about Wiley products, visit our web site at www.wiley.com.

Library of Congress Cataloging-in-Publication Data:

ISBN 0-471-27504-2

Printed in the United States of America.

10   9   8   7   6   5   4   3

To my wife, Jacqueline, my mother, Evelyn, and the memory of my father, Frank

—K.L.

For all those future speech-language pathologists. May wisdom and compassion guide all of your intervention decisions.

—J.V.W.

To my brother-in-law and coauthor, Keith Landis—a knowledgeable speech therapist and a very kind man of few words that are always well chosen.

—A.E.J.

CONTENTS

PRACTICE*PLANNERS*® SERIES PREFACE

The practice of psychotherapy, as well as other therapies, has a dimension that did not exist 30, 20, or even 15 years ago—accountability. Treatment programs, public agencies, clinics, and even group and solo practitioners must now justify the treatment of patients to outside review entities that control the payment of fees. This development has resulted in an explosion of paperwork. Clinicians must now document what has been done in treatment, what is planned for the future, and what the anticipated outcomes of the interventions are. The books and software in this Practice*Planners* series are designed to help practitioners fulfill these documentations requirements efficiently and professionally.

The Practice*Planners* series is growing rapidly. It now includes not only the original *The Complete Adult Psychotherapy Treatment Planner,* Third Edition, *The Child Psychotherapy Treatment Planner,* Third Edition, and *The Adolescent Psychotherapy Treatment Planner,* Third Edition, but also Treatment Planners targeted to specialty areas of practice, including: addictions, juvenile justice/residential care, couples therapy, employee assistance, behavioral medicine, therapy with older adults, pastoral counseling, family therapy, group therapy, neuropsychology, therapy with gays and lesbians, special education, school counseling, probation and parole, therapy with sexual abuse victims and offenders, and more.

Several of the Treatment Planner books now have companion Progress Notes Planners (e.g., Adult, Adolescent, Child, Addictions, Severe and Persistent Mental Illness, Couples). More of these planners, which provide a menu of progress statements that elaborate on the client's symptom presentation and the provider's therapeutic intervention are in production. Each Progress Notes Planner statement is directly integrated with "Behavioral Definitions" and "Therapeutic Interventions" items from the companion Treatment Planner.

The list of therapeutic Homework Planners is also growing from the original Brief Therapy Homework to Adult, Adolescent, Child, Couples, Group, Family, Addictions, Divorce, Grief, Employee Assistance, and School Counseling/School Social Work Homework Planners. Each of these books can be used alone or in conjunction with their companion Treatment Planner. Homework assignments are designed around each presenting problem (e.g., Anxiety, Depression, Chemical Dependence, Anger Management, Panic, Eating Disorders), which is the focus of a chapter in its corresponding Treatment Planner.

Client Education Handout Planners, a new branch in the series, provides brochures and handouts to help educate and inform adult, child, adolescent, couples, and family clients on a myriad of mental health issues, as well as life-skills techniques. The list of presenting problems for which information is provided mirrors the list of presenting problems in the Treatment Planner of the title similar to that of the Handout Planner. Thus, the problems for which educational material is provided in the *Child and Adolescent Client Education Handout Planner* reflect the presenting problems listed in *The Child* and The Adolescent Psychotherapy Treatment Planner books. Handouts are included on CD-ROMs for easy printing and are ideal for use in waiting rooms, at presentations, as newsletters, or as information for clients struggling with mental illness issues.

In addition, the series also includes Thera*Scribe*®, the latest version of the popular treatment planning, clinical record-keeping software. Thera-*Scribe* allows the user to import the data from any of the Treatment Planner, Progress Notes Planner, or Homework Planner books into the software's expandable database. Then the point-and-click method can create a detailed, neatly organized, individualized, and customized treatment plan along with optional integrated progress notes and homework assignments.

Adjunctive books, such as *The Psychotherapy Documentation Primer*, and *The Clinical, Forensic, Child, Couples and Family, Continuum of Care*, and *Chemical Dependence Documentation Sourcebook* contain forms and resources to aid the mental health practice management. The goal of the series is to provide practitioners with the resources they need to provide high-quality care in the era of accountability—or, to put it simply, we seek to help you spend more time on patients, and less time on paperwork.

ARTHUR E. JONGSMA, JR.
Grand Rapids, Michigan

ACKNOWLEDGMENTS

Many authors say that writing a book is a protracted exercise in loneliness. I am happy to report that this was not the case in the writing of this planner. From start to finish, I enjoyed the encouragement and support of several extraordinary people who made this project a truly collaborative effort. Indeed, without their help, I would not have had the stamina to see it to the end. Special thanks are due to Art Jongsma for proposing the project and guiding it, with great patience and good humor, to its conclusion. He is an ideal editor. Thanks are also due to Judy Vander Woude, an enviable combination of scholar and clinician. I learned greatly from her criticisms and insights, and I am a better clinician because of our collaboration. Jen Byrne's quietly meticulous work transformed my woeful attempts at word processing into beautifully readable text. Thanks, Jen. Finally, I would like to thank Peggy Alexander and the editorial staff at John Wiley & Sons for being willing to take a dare with this project, opening a new door for the *Treatment Planner Series*. Again, thank you all.

K.L.

A hearty thank you to Art Jongsma for his vision and patient editing of this project and to Jen Byrne, Dr. Jongsma's manuscript assistant, for keeping track of all those editorial changes with her always cheerful e-mails. A special note of gratitude to Keith Landis, whose expertise in adult and medical speech pathology complemented my work in the child and school-related areas. To my friends and colleagues who, as seasoned speech-language pathologists, provided invaluable feedback on the content of these chapters. Finally, I would like also to thank Peggy Alexander and the editorial staff at John Wiley & Sons for their willingness to enthusiastically support this work.

J.V.W.

Many thanks to Keith Landis and Judy Vander Woude for their fine work and openness to suggestions throughout the writing exercise. This was a true cooperative venture in which they led me through the maze of speech-language terms and therapeutic interventions while I shaped the content into our Practice*Planners* style and format.

Jen Byrne's skills continue to be indispensable in her manuscript preparation. Thanks again, Jen. David Bernstein has joined the editorial team at Wiley and I welcome him aboard. He joins Cris Wojdylo, Peggy Alexander, and Judi Knott, a support staff who have carried on the Practice*Planners* series most capably.

A.E.J.

INTRODUCTION

PLANNER FOCUS

The Speech-Language Pathology Treatment Planner is designed for speech-language pathologists who provide treatment for those with communication disorders. The *Planner* includes those areas most frequently recognized as our scope of practice by the American Speech-Language-Hearing Association. Although it is not an exhaustive list, the most common challenges for individuals with various communication disorders are addressed.

Interventions are designed to offer the speech-language pathologist a variety of functional and meaningful strategies to improve clients' communication skills. Emphasis is always on enhancing the strengths of clients and furthering their functional communication skills, regardless of the types and severities of their disability.

With the advent of managed care, treatment planning and outcome measurements are increasingly important in speech-language pathology practices. Managed care systems expect documented efficient and effective treatment for clients in a restricted time period. Treatment plans are expected to be well documented with clearly delineated outcomes. Speech-language pathologists in settings such as hospitals, home health care, rehabilitation, and private practice are expected to use effective high-quality treatment plans delivered in a relatively limited time frame. Our purpose in writing this book is to clarify, simplify, and accelerate the treatment planning process for novice speech-language pathologists and to remind more expert speech-language pathologists of best-practice assessment and intervention strategies and approaches.

TREATMENT PLAN UTILITY

Detailed, written treatment plans benefit not only the client, speech-language pathologist, rehabilitation team, insurance community, and

1

treatment agencies but also the overall speech pathology profession. The client is served by the written plan because it clearly outlines the essential outcomes of treatment. The client and significant others no longer wonder what the goals of therapy are; the client becomes an integral part of the treatment process by collaboratively designing the general treatment approach and specific goals with the speech-language pathologist. Both the client and the speech-language pathologist work with explicitly stated objectives and corresponding interventions. Most important, since needs can change as the client's circumstances change, the treatment plan must be viewed as a dynamic document that can, and must, be updated and adapted to address the client's specific communicative needs.

Clients and speech-language pathologists benefit from treatment plans because explicit plans force them to think carefully about therapy outcomes and ultimately be accountable for their time. Behaviorally stated, measurable objectives clearly focus the treatment endeavor. Clear objectives allow the client to channel effort into specific changes that will lead to the long-term goal of functional communication. Therapy is no longer a vague contract that seems to focus on meaningless discrete skills. Instead, both clients and speech-language pathologists are concentrating on explicitly stated objectives using specific interventions.

Speech-language pathologists are aided by treatment plans because they are forced to think analytically and critically about therapeutic interventions that are best suited to help clients attain objectives. Speech-language pathologists have always been trained to follow a formalized plan for the treatment process. Now this *Planner* will provide an easier way for speech-language pathologists to attend to the techniques, approaches, and measurable targets that form the basis for interventions.

Speech-language pathologists benefit also from clear documentation of treatment which provides a measure of added protection from possible client litigation. Malpractice suits are increasing in frequency, and insurance premiums are soaring. The first line of defense against allegations is a complete clinical record detailing the treatment process. The written, individualized, formal treatment plan, which is the guideline for intervention, that has been reviewed and signed by the clients and/or parents and coupled with problem-oriented progress notes is a powerful defense against exaggerated or false claims.

A well-crafted treatment plan that clearly stipulates presenting problems and intervention strategies facilitates the treatment process carried out by speech-language pathologists and other team members in a variety of treatment settings. Good communication among team members about implementation of approaches and responsibility for intervention is critical. A thorough treatment plan stipulates in writing the details of objectives, various interventions (individual therapy, group therapy, consultative, transdisciplinary, community or home-based, etc.) to be used and who will implement those interventions.

Every treatment agency or institution is constantly looking for ways to increase the quality and uniformity of documentation in the clinical record. The standardized, written treatment plan with problem definitions, goals, objectives, and interventions in every client's file enhances the uniformity of documentation and eases the task of record reviewers inside and outside agencies. The demand for accountability from third-party payers and health maintenance organizations is partially satisfied by the written treatment plan and progress notes. Managed care systems are demanding structured therapeutic contracts that have measurable objectives and explicit interventions. Speech-language pathologists cannot avoid the move toward being more accountable to those outside the treatment process.

The speech-language pathology profession stands to benefit from the use of precise, measurable objectives to evaluate success in treatment. With detailed treatment plans, outcome data can be more easily collected for interventions that are effective in achieving specific goals.

DEVELOPING A TREATMENT PLAN

The process of developing a treatment plan involves a logical series of steps that build on each other, much like constructing a house. The foundation of any effective treatment plan is the data gathered in a comprehensive transdisciplinary evaluation. As part of the process prior to developing the treatment plan, speech-language pathologists carefully listen to and understand the client's struggles with communication challenges, physical challenges, coping skills, self-esteem, family issues, social networks, occupational stressors, and so forth. The assessment data should be drawn from a variety of sources, which can include developmental and social history, standardized assessments, conversational samples, criterion-referenced evaluations, physical exams, clinical interviews, psychoeducational testing, psychiatric consultation, and medical consultations. The integration of the data by the speech-language pathologists and/or the transdisciplinary treatment team is critical for understanding the client and his or her needs. We have identified six specific steps for developing an effective treatment plan based on assessment data.

Step One: Problem Selection

Although the client and/or his or her parents may discuss a variety of issues during the assessment, the speech-language pathologists must focus the treatment process on the most significant problems. Usually, a *primary* deficit will surface, and *secondary* deficits may also be evident. *Other* problems may have to be set aside as not urgent enough to require simultaneous treatment. An effective treatment plan can deal with only a few selected deficits at a time or treatment will lose its direction. A variety of specific speech and language disorders are presented as chapter titles within *The Speech-Language Pathology Treatment Planner.* The speech-language pathologists may select disorders that most accurately represent the client's current needs.

It is important to consider the opinions of clients (as appropriate, depending on the client's age and mental status) and significant others to prioritize communicative issues and other related disabilities. A client's motivation to participate in and cooperate with the treatment process depends, to some extent, on the degree to which treatment addresses his or her greatest needs and how treatment goals directly relate to improvements in his or her communication in everyday life.

Step Two: Problem Definition

Each individual client presents with unique characteristics that reveal how a problem behaviorally impacts communication in his or her life. Therefore, each problem that is selected for treatment focus requires a specific definition about how it is evidenced in that particular client. Turn to the chapter that best describes the identified or suspected disability of the client. Select the statements from the behavioral definitions listed at the beginning of the chapter that appear most descriptive of the client's needs.

Step Three: Goal Development

The next step in treatment plan development is setting broad goals for the resolution of the target communicative problem. The statements need not be crafted in measurable terms but can be global, long-term goals that indicate the desired positive outcomes of treatment. The *Planner* suggests several possible goal statements for each problem, but only one statement is required in a treatment plan.

Step Four: Objective Construction

In contrast to long-term goals, short-term objectives must be stated in behaviorally measurable language. It must be clear when the client has achieved the established objectives; therefore vague, subjective objectives are not acceptable. The objectives presented in this *Planner* are designed to meet the demand for measurable objectives that lead to measurable treatment outcomes. Alternatives are presented to allow construction of a variety of treatment plan possibilities for the same presenting problem. The speech-language pathologists must exercise professional judgment concerning objectives that are most appropriate for a given client.

Each objective should be developed into a step toward attaining the broad treatment goal. In essence, objectives can be thought of as a series of steps that, when completed, will result in the achievement of the long-term goal. There should be at least two objectives for each problem, but the clinician may construct as many as necessary for goal achievement. Target attainment dates may be listed for each objective. New objectives should be added to the plan as the individual's treatment progresses. When all the necessary objectives have been achieved, the client should have resolved the target deficit successfully.

Step Five: Intervention Creation

Interventions are the actions of the speech-language pathologists designed to help the client complete the objectives. There should be at least one intervention for every objective. If the client does not accomplish the objective after the initial intervention, new interventions should be added to plan.

Interventions should be selected on the basis of the client's needs and drawn from the speech-language pathologist's full therapeutic repertoire. This *Planner* contains interventions from a broad range of therapeutic approaches, including cognitive, dynamic, behavioral, or family-oriented approaches. Many interventions are based on the published work of other professionals. We gave credit to those professionals for their intervention suggestions in the annotated bibliography in Appendix A, which is organized by disability or disorder. Other interventions may be written by the speech-language pathologists to reflect his or her training and experience. The addition of new problems, definitions, goals, objectives, and interventions to those found in the *Planner* is encouraged to add to the database for future reference and use.

Some suggested interventions listed in this *Planner* refer to specific books that can be provided to the client or the client's parents for additional information, as located in Appendix B.

Step Six: Diagnosis Determination

The determination of an appropriate diagnosis is based on an evaluation of the client's complete clinical presentation. The speech-language pathologist must compare the client's communicative, behavioral, cognitive, emotional, and physical symptoms to the criteria for diagnosis of a communication disorder condition as described in *DSM-IV-TR*. Diagnosis is a reality that exists in the world of health care, and it is a necessity for third-party reimbursement. Recently, managed care agencies are more interested in behavioral indices that are exhibited by the client than in the actual diagnosis.

Several speech-language disabilities or disorders do not have specific *DSM-IV-TR* conditions and, thus, have been listed as Communication Disorder Not Otherwise Specified (NOS). Even so, the speech pathologist's complete understanding of the client assessment data will contribute to the most reliable, valid diagnosis. An accurate assessment of behavioral indicators will also contribute to more effective treatment planning.

HOW TO USE THIS PLANNER

The Speech-Language Pathology Treatment Planner was developed as a tool to aid speech-language pathologists in writing a treatment plan that is clear, specific, and highly individualized according to the following progression:

1. Choose one presenting problem (Step One) you have identified through a preliminary assessment process. Locate the corresponding page number for the problem in the *Planner's* table of contents.
2. Select two or three of the listed behavioral definitions (Step Two) and record them in the appropriate section on your treatment plan form. Feel free to add your own definitions if you determine that your client's behavioral manifestation of the identified problem is not listed.
3. Select a single long-term goal (Step Three) and again write the selection, as it written in the *Planner,* or in a modified form, in the corresponding area of your own treatment form.
4. Review the listed objectives for this problem and select the ones that you judge to be clinically indicated for your client (Step Four). Remember, it is recommended that you select at least two objectives for each problem. Add a target date or the number of sessions allocated for the attainment of each objective.
5. Choose relevant interventions (Step Five). The *Planner* offers suggested interventions related to each objective in parentheses following the objective statement, but do not limit yourself to those interventions. The entire list is eclectic and may offer options that are more tailored to your theoretical approach or preferred way of working with clients. You may refer also to the annotated bibliography at the end of the *Planner* for additional sources related to the

interventions. Also, just as with definitions, goals, and objectives, there is space for you to enter your own interventions into the *Planner.* This allows you to refer to these entries when you create a plan around this problem in the future. If treatment is implemented by a transdisciplinary team, it is important to collaboratively assign responsibility for implementation of each intervention.

6. Several *DSM-IV-TR* diagnoses are listed at the end of each chapter that are commonly associated with a client who has a particular disorder. Select a diagnosis listed or assign a more appropriate choice from the *DSM-IV-TR* (Step Six). Some disorders may present multiple diagnoses. If so, refer to each chapter that addresses the specific diagnoses.

Congratulations! You now have a complete, individualized treatment plan that is ready for immediate implementation and presentation to the client. It should resemble the format of the "Sample Treatment Plan" at the end of this chapter.

A FINAL NOTE

One important aspect of effective treatment planning is that each plan should be tailored to the individual client's needs. Treatment plans should not be mass produced, even if clients have similar disorders. The individual's strengths and weaknesses, unique stressors, community and cultural norms, and ethnic backgrounds *must* be considered in developing a treatment strategy. Drawing on our own years of clinical experience, we have put together a variety of treatment choices. These statements can be combined in thousands of permutations to develop detailed treatment plans. Relying on their own professional judgment, speech-language pathologists can easily select the statements that are appropriate for the individuals they are treating. In addition, we encourage you to add your own definitions, goals, objectives, and interventions to the existing samples. It is our hope that *The Speech-Language Pathology Treatment Planner* will benefit the client, the speech-language pathologist, and the speech pathology profession.

SUMMARY

Our experience has taught us that learning the skills of effective treatment-plan writing can be a tedious process for many speech-language pathologists. It is stressful to develop this expertise when under the pressure of increased client loads and short time frames placed on speech pathologists today by managed care systems and schools with increased financial burdens. The documentation demands can be overwhelming when we must move quickly from assessment to treatment plans to progress notes. In the process, we must be specific about how and when objectives can be achieved and how progress is exhibited in each client. We have put together a variety of choices to allow for thousands of potential combinations of statements that join to make a complete plan for treatment. Speech-language pathologists, with their good judgment, can easily select statements that are appropriate for the individuals they are treating. Each statement can be modified as necessary to apply more directly to a specific client. Finally, we believe from our experience that the *Planner* method is helpful in that it stimulates speech-language pathologists' creativity. New ideas for all components of a treatment plan may come to mind as the *Planner* statements are reviewed. Speech-language pathologists can add to the *Planner* by writing in new definitions, goals, objectives, and interventions to develop effective treatment strategies.

SAMPLE TREATMENT PLAN

PROBLEM: PHONOLOGICAL DISORDER

Definitions: Overall phonological production is substantially below expected phonological developmental norms.

Consistent and significant difficulty producing phonemes in different positions within words, phrases, and/or sentences.

Spontaneous speech is consistently judged to be unintelligible by unfamiliar adults.

Production of phonemes in conversations interferes significantly with effective communication at home, school, and community.

Goals: Produce phonemes in different communicative contexts appropriate for age, cognition, physical ability, and dialect.

Clear intelligibility when communicating with others at home, school, and in the community.

Develop understanding of the phonological features of language.

Parents establish realistic expectations for their child's phonological skills and work collaboratively with the speech-language pathologist (SLP) to develop effective treatment strategies.

OBJECTIVES

1. Participate willingly in a phonological assessment.

INTERVENTIONS

1. Administer a phonological processes test to evaluate the client's error patterns (e.g., final-consonant deletion, initial-consonant deletion, cluster simplification, velar fronting, gliding, depalatization, deaffrication, or fronting).

2. Videotape a conversational speech sample that represents the client's typical connected speech production while playing with

interactive toys or discussing favorite television shows, movies, books, or games; analyze the tape for his/her phonological production.

3. Establish a measurable baseline of the client's phonological skills before treatment begins.

2. Parents and the client, if age-appropriate, participate in the evaluation process and contribute to the interpretation of evaluation information.

1. Ask the parents and the client, if age-appropriate, to provide information on his/her developmental milestones, current medical status and history, previous professional intervention, phonological production in the home, and relevant social and family concerns.

3. Parents and the client, if age-appropriate, accept the recommendations given and collaboratively select phonological targets and a general intervention strategy.

1. Conduct a meeting with the parents and the client, if age-appropriate, first, to determine his/her eligibility for services and, second, to develop collaborative intervention strategies.

2. Select specific phonemes or phonological processes as targets for intervention based on the child's age, stimulability, intelligibility, dialect, and/or social and educational communicative needs.

4. Participate willingly in an audiological evaluation.

1. Conduct a pure-tone audiological screening at 500 Hz, 1000 Hz, 2000 Hz, and 4000 Hz at 20 dB for children and 25 dB for adults.

2. Refer the client to an audiologist for a complete evaluation if results of the audiological screening indicate a need for further assessment.

5. Increase intelligibility to 80% by reducing phonological processes, as judged by the SLP.

1. If the client is highly unintelligible, select a cycles-intervention approach to target identified phonological processes: (1) read a

word list with amplification that highlights specific phonological processes used by the client, (2) ask the client to color and paste three to five pictures of carefully selected words, (3) help the client say the words on the picture cards, (4) assess the client's stimulability for other phonemes, and (5) read the same word list again.

6. Parents take an active role in working positively with their child on daily 10-minute phonological exercises.

1. Maintain ongoing, frequent contact with the parents, discussing specific methods for eliciting phonological productions and reporting progress or concerns regarding the client's phonological needs.

2. Ask the parents to read lists of 10 to 12 words to the client every day that contain specific phonemes that illustrate his/her targeted phonological processes.

7. Pronounce target phonemes accurately and consistently in different communicative situations, as judged by the client's teachers, parents, and peers.

1. Survey the client's parents, teachers, and significant others to determine whether he/she is using the target phonemes accurately in daily conversations.

Diagnosis: 315.39 Phonological Disorder

ACCENT REDUCTION

BEHAVIORAL DEFINITIONS

1. Non-native speakers of American English who have difficulty producing specific English phonemes in different positions within words, phrases, and/or sentences.
2. Good American English vocabulary and syntax skills.
3. Difficulty with suprasegmental features of American English words and phrases.
4. Omission of American English morphemes.
5. Difficulty with American English cultural rules of communication.
6. Speech production in conversations interferes significantly with effective communication at school, work, and/or in the community.

__. _____

_____

__. _____

_____

__. _____

_____

LONG-TERM GOALS

1. Produce American English phonemes correctly in different communicative contexts.
2. Clear intelligibility when speaking in American English with others at school, work, and in the community.
3. Understand the phonological features of American English.
4. Understand the phonological differences between the client's first language and English sounds.

5. Produce intonational features of the American English language appropriately in different communicative situations.
6. Implement the cultural rules of using American English in different communicative contexts.

___. _____
_____
___. _____
_____
___. _____
_____

SHORT-TERM OBJECTIVES

1. Participate willingly in an assessment. (1, 2, 3, 4)

THERAPEUTIC INTERVENTIONS

1. Administer the *Proficiency in Oral English Communication* (Sikorski) to determine the client's articulation, auditory discrimination, intonation, syntax, vocabulary, and pragmatic language skills in American English.

2. Videotape conversational speech samples that represent the client's typical American English speech production; analyze his/her American English proficiency by noting features such as phoneme production, body language, syntax, and intonation.

3. Ask the client to provide information on his/her background (e.g., how long he/she has been speaking English, native language and dialect, academic and work history; previous professional intervention and relevant social, academic, and occupational concerns).

4. Establish a measurable base line of the client's English speaking skills before treatment begins.

2. Cooperate with an oral-motor examination. (5)

5. Evaluate the client's oral-motor skills by first observing the visible structure of his/her face, lips, teeth, tongue, and hard and soft palate and then assess how he/she uses specific structures important for speech production (e.g., movement, strength, and closure of the lips; strength, protrusion, retraction, and lateralization of the tongue; or movement of the soft palate when producing the /a/ phoneme).

3. Participate willingly in an audiological evaluation. (6, 7)

6. Conduct a pure-tone audi-ological screening at 500 Hz, 1000 Hz, 2000 Hz, and 4000 Hz at 20 dB for children and 25 dB for adults (see *Guidelines for Audiologic Screening* by American Speech-Language-Hearing Association).

7. Refer the client to an audiologist for a complete evaluation if results of the audiological screening indicate a need for further assessment.

4. Accept the recommendations given, and collaboratively select specific goals and a general intervention strategy. (8, 9, 10)

8. Conduct a meeting with the client, first, to review assessment results and, second, to develop collaborative goals and intervention strategies.

9. Determine the most appropriate general therapeutic approach by considering key linguistic and cultural differences between the client's native language and American English.

5. Verbalize an understanding of how specific therapeutic interventions contribute to better American English speaking skills. (11,12)

10. Select specific phonemes as targets for intervention based on the client's accent.

11. Before beginning an activity, clearly state the therapeutic goal of the activity for the client and again, at the end of the activity, ask him/her to state the specific goal for that activity.

12. Help the client chart therapeutic progress by indicating accomplishments on a visual aid illustrating the sequential stages necessary for achieving long-term goals.

6. Discriminate between two words with minimally different phonetic sounds with 90% accuracy. (13, 14, 15)

13. Instruct the client to choose the pictures that represent the words that he/she hears when shown pictures of minimal pair words (e.g., "me" or "meet") that highlight his/her target phonemes (e.g., /l/ and /r/).

14. Provide the client with audiotapes or Internet web sites that have lists of minimally contrasting words to practice discriminating between minimally different sounds (see *Listening Comprehension Exercises* by Beare at http:esl.about.com).

15. Assist the client in determining whether target sounds occur in the initial prevocalic, medial intervocalic, or final postvocalic positions of words (e.g., ask if the /l/ sound in "yellow" is at the beginning, middle, or end of the word).

7. Practice listening and speaking exercises 10- to 30-minutes daily, as directed by the SLP. (16)

16. Give the client exercises (e.g., listening to word lists and repeating words and sentences) to practice with an audio recorder.

8. Identify correct American English productions with 90% accuracy. (17, 18)

17. Say the client's incorrect patterns of speech production purposefully on some of the words in a familiar short story and instruct him/her to listen carefully and say, "I heard it!" after hearing the incorrect production.

18. While viewing video recordings of the client practicing intervention strategies, ask the client to identify his/her correct and incorrect American English productions.

9. Make the correct articulatory placement for American English phonemes. (19, 20, 21)

19. Use mirrors and tongue blades or cotton swab sticks to provide detailed kinesthetic and visual cues to position the client's lips, teeth, and/or tongue for target phonemes.

20. Present pictures, diagrams, or computer simulations of the positions of the articulators to the client as models of the placement needed for specific phonemes.

21. Use phonemes with similar distinctive features to elicit target phonemes (e.g., ask the client to repeat the aspirated /t/ phoneme quickly to produce the /s/ phoneme); point out that the articulator positions are similar.

10. Pronounce American English phonemes correctly in words with 90% accuracy. (22, 23, 24, 25)

22. Provide practice on phonemes that are difficult for the client to pronounce.

23. Provide practice on target phonemes in phrases or short sentences by using slow-motion speech, echo speech, unison speaking, or role playing.

24. Teach the client phonetic symbols and features, so he/she will

understand the placement, manner, and voicing features of American English sounds and to enable him/her to look up pronunciations of unfamiliar words in American English dictionaries (refer the client to *Reference and Introduction to Phonetic Symbols* by Beare at http://esl.about.com/library /weekly/aa040998.htm).

25. Teach the client the use of unstressed vowels, less intensity, and lowered pitch for the pronunciation of unstressed syllables in words and phrases.

11. Pronounce American phonemes correctly in common phrases and sentences with 80% accuracy. (26, 27, 28)

26. Have the client read or tell jokes and riddles using correct phonological productions of the target phonemes.

27. Help the client practice common phrases he/she would use in his/her occupation and/or in social situations.

28. Monitor and correct the client's speech production during conversations by asking leading questions: (a) "Tell me about your favorite movie or television show," (b) "If you won a million dollars, what would you do?"or (c) "What did you do during your vacation?"

12. Use stress and unstressed words correctly in sentences with 90% accuracy. (29, 30)

29. Teach the difference between content words (e.g., nouns, verbs, and adjectives) that are generally stressed, and function words (e.g., prepositions, auxiliaries, pronouns, and articles) that are usually unstressed.

30. Teach the client how using stress contrastively on different

content words in a sentence creates subtle changes in meaning for the listener.

13. Use rate and pitch correctly in different situations to convey different meanings. (31, 32, 33)

31. Teach the client how the prosodic features of pitch, intensity, and rate affect the meaning and emotional interest of what is spoken.

32. Model various intonation patterns (e.g., declarative statements, question forms, embedded phrases); have the client mark a reading passage with varying intonation patterns and then read the passage; critique him/her on the effectiveness of his/her expression.

33. Count the number of words the client reads in one minute; have him/her adjust his/her rate by using a stopwatch when reading and bringing the rate into the 150 to 180 words per minute range, which is typical for speakers of American English.

14. Use American English morphemes correctly with 90% accuracy. (34)

34. Teach the client various morphemes (e.g., regular and irregular plurals, regular and irregular past tense markers); provide him/her with word lists to study; engage him/her in conversation and randomly insert errors of usage (e.g., "I goed away") while talking; ask the client to listen for errors and note them by holding up a finger, then ask him/her to say the word in its correct form.

15. Learn American English pragmatic conversational strategies. (35)

35. Teach the client how to manage interruptions (e.g., "excuse me"), revise messages if misunderstood, and appropriately

use American English nonverbal cues (e.g., eye contact, gestures, and proximity) to the listener.

—. _____   —. _____
      _____   _____
—. _____   —. _____
      _____   _____
—. _____   —. _____
      _____   _____

DIAGNOSTIC SUGGESTIONS:

Axis I: 307.9   Communication Disorder NOS

_____   _____

_____   _____

ALARYNGEAL SPEECH

BEHAVIORAL DEFINITIONS

1. Surgical removal of the larynx.
2. Inability to produce laryngeal vibration for voicing.
3. Surgical alteration of the respiratory tract resulting in breathing accomplished via a stoma in the neck.

—. _____
   _____
   _____

—. _____
   _____
   _____

—. _____
   _____

LONG-TERM GOALS

1. Consistently use a nonlaryngeal means of achieving voice for communication in a variety of situations.
2. Effectively use nonverbal communication strategies with alaryngeal speech to reinforce the emotional content of speech.
3. Demonstrate proper self-care of the stoma and/or tracheal prosthesis.

—. _____
   _____
   _____

—. _____
   _____
   _____

—. _____
   _____

SHORT-TERM OBJECTIVES

1. Willingly participate in pre-surgery education and counseling. (1, 2)

2. Maintain proper hygiene of the stoma. (3, 4)

3. Practice safety precautions relevant to neck breathing. (5)

THERAPEUTIC INTERVENTIONS

1. Visit the client prior to surgery and provide support and information regarding the laryngectomy and postsurgical concerns, including the loss of voice, alterations in the breathing mechanism, and alternatives for vocal rehabilitation; if possible, invite a client who has successfully undergone laryngectomy and vocal rehabilitation to meet with the client and his/her family to give a personal account of surgery, recovery, issues of grief and loss, and vocal restoration.

2. Confer with the medical/surgical team regarding matters that will impact the client's vocal rehabilitation (e.g., the extent of the surgery, the client's respiratory status postsurgery, and the possible need for additional medical intervention such as radiation therapy).

3. Educate the client in the structure and functioning of his/her altered respiratory system, explaining that his/her breathing no longer occurs through the mouth and nose but through an opening (stoma) in the neck.

4. Reinforce instruction given by the nurse and respiratory therapist in the proper suctioning and cleaning of the stoma.

5. Instruct the client in safety measures relevant to stoma breathing (e.g., avoiding

extremes in temperature and blowing debris that may enter the stoma, ensuring proper levels of humidity, and exercising precautions during water sports and swimming to prevent water from entering the stoma).

4. Participate in the vocal rehabilitation assessment and accept recommendations for vocal restoration. (6)

6. Determine the most appropriate method of vocal restoration for the client—pharyngeal phonation, mechanically derived vibration for voicing, or prosthetic/surgical intervention.

5. Inhale air into the esophagus with 95% effectiveness. (7)

7. Teach the client the inhalation method of esophageal air intake by asking him/her to sniff air into the esophagus while quickly jerking the head back to trap air in the upper part of the esophagus and then releasing the air in a burp.

6. Produce speech using pharyngeal vibration for voicing with 95% effectiveness. (8, 9, 10, 11)

8. After production of the burp is established, teach the client to shape the sound into vowels.

9. Teach the client to combine the vowel sounds with initial consonants to make syllables.

10. Teach the client to shape the syllable sounds into words and then extend the words into verbalization of short phrases.

11. Teach the client to integrate meaningful communicative units of two or three words per each burp into short conversation.

7. Inject air into the esophagus to produce pharyngeal vibration for speech. (12, 13)

12. Teach the client to inject air into the esophagus using the glossopharyngeal press by asking him/her to position the tongue firmly on the alveolar ridge and move the tongue backward like a plunger, forcing air into the

esophagus and then releasing the air in a burp.

13. Teach the client to shape the burp into vowel sounds, to combine vowel sounds with initial consonants, to extend syllables into words and short phrases, and then to produce meaningful units of two or three words per burp.

8. Carry out consonantal injection of air into the esophagus to produce pharyngeal vibration for speech. (14, 15, 16)

14. Teach the client consonantal air injection techniques by asking him/her to force air into the esophagus on speech sounds, especially initial plosives (e.g., /t/, /d/, /p/).

15. Coach the client in the practice of repeating syllables of initial plosives combined with vowels in quick succession (e.g., /ta-ta-ta/).

16. Teach the client to use consonantal injection in connected speech; reinforce efforts and successes and redirect for failure.

9. Produce buccal vibration as the sound source for speech with 85% intelligibility. (17, 18)

17. Teach the client to vibrate the lateral portions of the tongue against the side teeth, amplifying the vibration in the buccal cavities, to produce a Donald Duck-like sound.

18. Practice the production of syllables, words, and phrases with the client using buccal vibration as the sound source for speech.

10. Produce velar vibration as a sound source for speech. (19, 20, 21)

19. Ask the client to vibrate his/her velum against the base of the tongue to produce a fricative sound.

20. Teach the client the production of syllables, words, and phrases using velar vibration as the sound source for speech.

21. Use modeling and behavior rehearsal to teach the client how to combine the techniques of buccal and velar speech for communication; reinforce for positive effort and success, as well as redirect for failures.

11. Locate the most effective placement of the electrolarynx. (22, 23)

22. Present the client with a variety of electrolarynges and demonstrate their use.

23. Demonstrate the most effective placement of the electrolarynx on the client's neck or under the chin, emphasizing the importance of maintaining firm contact of the device against the neck.

12. Use the electrolarynx with exaggerated articulatory movements. (24, 25, 26)

24. Teach the client to activate the electrolarynx while he/she holds it firmly against the neck.

25. Model and engage in behavior rehearsal of the use of the electrolarynx to produce hard articulatory contact of plosives and forceful production of fricatives using residual air in the oral cavity to increase intelligibility.

26. Teach the client to speak with his/her mouth wide open to increase oral resonance when using the electrolarynx.

13. Coordinate the activation of the electrolarynx with exaggerated articulation to produce short, intelligible phrases with 95% effectiveness. (27, 28, 29, 30)

27. Ask the client to activate the electrolarynx and orally produce isolated vowels while maintaining a steady vibration of the device, using good placement.

28. Teach the client to coordinate activation to the electrolarynx with overarticulated oral movements to combine the vibrating sound source with articulation.

29. Ask the client to say automatized sequences (e.g., numbers, day of the week) while maintaining steady activation of the device.

30. Ask the client to say short, meaningful phrases while correctly combining activation of the electrolarynx with overarticulation.

14. Enhance the degree of emotional expression using nonverbal strategies with 90% effectiveness. (31, 32)

31. Teach the client to counter the mechanical sound of the electrolarynx and enhance emotional expression by varying the rate of speech and phrasing and introducing pauses into conversation.

32. Encourage the client to speak with exaggerated facial expressions to reinforce the emotional content of what he/she is saying.

15. Take steps to help listeners become more comfortable with electrolaryngeal speech. (33, 34)

33. Instruct the client in nonverbal strategies to enhance the flow of conversation (e.g., taking the electrolarynx away from the neck to indicate a pause; holding the device to the neck to indicate that something is to be said).

34. Encourage the client to explain the device and its use when encountering strangers to reduce their distraction during conversation.

16. Achieve voicing for speech following surgical/prosthetic intervention. (35, 36, 37, 38)

35. Provide input to the medical/surgical team regarding the client's alertness, cognition, motivation, and potential for administering self-care; accept

the team's recommendation regarding the most appropriate type of prosthetic device to be used (e.g., the Blom-Singer tracheoesophageal voice prosthesis or the Voice Button prosthesis).

36. Instruct the client in the functioning, hygiene, and insertion and removal of the prosthesis according to the medical team's recommendations.

37. Assist the medical team in troubleshooting problems, such as leakage around the prosthesis, mobility of the prosthesis valve, and the client's respiratory status. (*Note:* Specialized training is required for the SLP to participate in the management of tracheoesophageal prostheses.)

38. Teach the client to occlude the stoma and produce /a/; after stabilization of the /a/ has been achieved, extend vocal production to words, phrases, and sentences.

17. Utilize the newly established voicing procedures and techniques in a variety of social situations. (39)

39. Accompany the client on outings away from the therapy room to reinforce the voicing strategies learned in therapy in everyday situations.

__. _____
   _____

__. _____
   _____

__. _____
   _____

__. _____
   _____

__. _____
   _____

__. _____
   _____

DIAGNOSTIC SUGGESTIONS:

Axis I: 307.9   Communication Disorder NOS
V71.09   No Diagnosis

_____   _____

_____   _____

APHASIA

BEHAVIORAL DEFINITIONS

1. Slow, labored, halting speech consisting primarily of content words; functor words, such as articles and prepositions, are few (telegraphic speech).
2. Difficulty with word retrieval.
3. Fluent, grammatically correct speech containing many semantic errors (empty speech) or containing neologistic jargon (speech is incomprehensible).
4. Fluent speech containing literal and/or verbal paraphasias.
5. Auditory comprehension skills are impaired, as manifested in difficulties following directions, recognizing spoken words, and answering question forms accurately.
6. Verbal repetition skills are poor.
7. Extended latencies in processing auditory information or initiating oral expression.
8. Fluent/hyperfluent, circumlocuitous speech lacking in content words (anomic speech).
9. Issues stereotypic utterances.
10. Nonsymbolic disturbances (i.e., agnosia, apraxia, or perseveration) are present.

__. _____

_____

__. _____

_____

__. _____

_____

LONG-TERM GOALS

1. Improve auditory comprehension skills to level of potential.
2. Improve verbal expression to level of potential.
3. Consistently use self-cueing and prompting strategies to maintain communication skills at level of potential.
4. Family/caregiver demonstrates understanding of client's communication deficits.
5. Family/caregiver implements a communication carry-over program after the conclusion of formal therapy.

—. _____

_____

—. _____

_____

—. _____

_____

SHORT-TERM OBJECTIVES

1. Cooperate with a medical/ neurological evaluation. (1, 2)

2. Participate in the speech-language evaluation. (3)

3. Participate with family/ caregivers in a meeting to present evaluation results and proposals for an intervention strategy. (4)

THERAPEUTIC INTERVENTIONS

1. Confer with the medical team regarding the client's current diagnosis, medical history, previous treatment, and rehabilitative potential.

2. Discuss with the client and family the medical team's findings and the implications of the medical condition for speech and language.

3. Conduct the speech-language evaluation focusing on aphasia deficits.

4. Arrange an interpretive staffing meeting with the client's family to discuss the findings of the evaluation, the prognosis for recovery of communication skills, and an intervention strategy.

4. Parents/caregivers provide information regarding the client's history and current level of functioning. (5)

5. Maintain attention to the tasks assigned by the SLP. (6, 7, 8)

6. Carry out purposeful responses to visual stimuli. (9, 10)

7. Demonstrate increased comprehension of single words with 90% accuracy by pointing to pictures or objects as they are named. (11, 12)

5. Gather input from the client's family/caregivers regarding his/her level of education, occupation, communicative sophistication, and functional communication needs at home.

6. Establish consistent eye contact and appropriate physical proximity to the client.

7. Reflect the client's affect and assure the client that his/her affect is understood (e.g., "I see that you're frustrated").

8. Positively acknowledge the client's attempts to communicate (e.g., " I can see that you are really trying to talk," and "That is difficult for you").

9. To increase focus and awareness of visual stimuli, implement the beginning stages of visual action therapy (VAT) by having the client finger-trace line drawings, manipulate functional objects, and match objects to line drawings.

10. Present the client with a variety of pictures and objects, modeling the production of the words and demonstrate, using gestures, the functions of the objects; encourage the client to imitate.

11. Present the client with pictures or objects in a specified field, asking him/her to point to the correct picture/object after it is named; reinforce success and increase the number of pictures/objects as he/she shows improvement.

12. Ask the client to point to objects around the room, increasing the

number of objects per command (e.g., "Point to the ceiling" or "Point to the ceiling and then to the window"); reinforce correct responding.

8. Produce any type of verbal output. (13)

13. Model isolated vowel sounds and consonant-vowel and vowel-consonant combinations, using a mirror and motokinesthetic methods; encourage the client to imitate.

9. Increase the variety and amount of verbal output. (14, 15)

14. Model automatized verbal sequences (e.g., numbers, days of the week, months), familiar simple songs, or the client's personal identifying information; encourage the client to imitate.

15. To facilitate verbal output, hum a brief melodic pattern to the client (e.g., three notes), add words to the melodic pattern (e.g., "How are you?"), sing the utterance to him/her, fade the melodic pattern until the words are spoken only; elicit the client's verbal imitation at each step and reinforce success.

10. Correctly carry out basic auditory commands with 90% accuracy. (16)

16. Combine auditory commands with gestures or hand-over-hand prompts, gradually reducing the number of prompts until the client carries out the commands when given only verbal input.

11. Improve word retrieval skills. (17, 18)

17. Devise and present a hierarchy of cues to facilitate the client's word retrieval, including carrier phrases, first phoneme cues, word association cues, and function cues, gradually reducing the number of cues needed for him/her to retrieve target words.

18. Facilitate the client's word retrieval using tasks such as picture naming, responsive naming, sentence completion, object-attribute and function, word association, and categorization.

12. Indicate correct yes/no responses to basic question forms with 90% accuracy. (19)

19. Present the client with questions regarding personal information and the immediate environment, praising correct responses; if he/she gives an incorrect response, simply give the correct one and proceed to the next question.

13. Combine spoken words into phrases. (20)

20. Using words the client has learned previously, combine them with articles, prepositions, adjectives, and verbs to make grammatical units, asking the client to repeat these phrases.

14. Carry out complex auditory commands with 90% accuracy. (12, 21)

12. Ask the client to point to objects around the room, increasing the number of objects per command (e.g., "Point to the ceiling," "Point to the ceiling then to the window"); reinforce correct responding.

21. Demonstrate two- and three-step commands, combining commands with functional objects (e.g., "Pick up the glass and put it on the tray"); gradually eliminate the demonstrations until the client can carry out the commands given only auditory input.

15. Indicate correct yes/no responses to complex question forms with 90% accuracy. (22)

22. Present the client with a picture and a short series of spoken questions, asking him/her to respond with "Yes" or "No" after the presentation of each item.

16. Answer questions accurately to demonstrate verbalized comprehension of basic content presented in auditory form. (23, 24)

17. Combine spoken words into sentences. (25)

18. Demonstrate verbalized comprehension of detailed content presented in auditory and/or written form. (26, 27)

19. Increase the informational content of spoken sentences. (28, 29)

23. Read a selection of two or three sentences from a story to the client, asking questions about significant events, people, or places in the selection; reinforce accurate answers.

24. Ask the client to watch a brief segment of a television program that interests him/her; ask questions about significant people, events, or places in the program; reinforce accurate comprehension.

25. Present the client with action pictures taken from magazines, newspapers, or other sources; ask him/her to describe what is happening in the pictures.

26. Read passages to the client, watch brief segments of television programs together, or listen to brief radio selections together; ask him/her questions about minor events, people, or places from the selections.

27. Assign the client a brief newspaper or magazine article to read and then ask him/her questions about minor events, people, or places in the articles to confirm that the content was understood.

28. Ask the client a series of conversational questions, encouraging him/her to answer in complete sentences (e.g., Q: "How old are you?" A: "I'm seventy-five." Q: "What meal do you eat in the morning?" A: "I eat breakfast").

29. Engage in structured conversation with the client,

discussing topics that he/she finds interesting; ask leading questions to elicit increasing amounts of information from him/her.

20. Reduce the frequency of production of extraneous verbalizations, such as neologisms, paraphasias, and perseverations. (30)

30. Instruct the client in self-cueing techniques, including functional description, gestural prompts directed at the listener to help provide a word, carrier phrases (e.g., "I'm thinking of the word ____"), or written self-cues.

21. Demonstrate comprehension of speech at the conversational level by accurately answering questions regarding verbally presented content. (31, 32)

31. Present extended, complex written material of topical interest to the client for him/her to read; ask questions targeted at increasing the retention of information and then expressing himself/herself in extended utterances.

32. Listen to radio programs or watch television shows with the client; ask questions targeted at increasing retention of information and expressing himself/herself in extended utterances.

22. Expand the use of appropriate grammatical structures in spoken sentences. (33)

33. Ask the client questions to elicit targeted grammatical constructs (e.g., target construct: prepositional phrase—Q: "Where do you keep the dishes?" A: " *In* the cabinet." See Exhibits 5-11 and 5-12 in Burns and Halpen).

23. Engage in speech at the conversational level. (32, 34, 35)

32. Listen to radio programs or watch television shows with the client; ask questions targeted at having him/her retain increasing amounts of information and express himself/herself in extended utterances.

34. Role-play specific conversational situations (e.g., ordering at a restaurant or calling the doctor), targeting efficiency and clarity of expression; reinforce the client's successes.

35. Assign the client to attend specific facility-based activities; at the next treatment session, have him/her recount what transpired at the activity.

24. Use self-cueing and compensatory strategies to maintain communication skills. (36, 37)

36. Involve the client in a group therapy session with other clients who have aphasia; during the session, emphasize topic maintenance and his/her use of self-cueing techniques.

37. Instruct the client in the consistent use of strategies, including circumlocutions, structured pauses, and repetition of previous phrases, to compensate for word retrieval difficulties and to enhance the flow of conversation.

25. Consistently use the strategies and techniques developed for a home carry-over program. (38)

38. Develop a carry-over program (to be used when the client returns home) that includes the types of cues, compensatory strategies, and facilitative techniques that are most effective in maintaining the client's communication skills; instruct his/her family/caregiver in the implementation of the program.

__. _____   __. _____
    _____   _____
__. _____   __. _____
    _____   _____
__. _____   __. _____
    _____   _____

DIAGNOSTIC SUGGESTIONS:

Axis I:	294.9	Cognitive Disorder NOS
	294.8	Dementia NOS
	315.31	Expressive Language Disorder
	307.9	Communication Disorder NOS
	315.39	Phonological Disorder
	_____	_____
	_____	_____

APRAXIA

BEHAVIORAL DEFINITIONS

1. Slow, labored, hesitant speech with observable struggle and groping of the oral structures.
2. Oral motor exam does not reveal muscular weakness, slowness, or incoordination.
3. Inconsistent, unpredictable articulation errors.
4. More frequent articulation errors on fricatives, affricates, and consonant clusters than on vowels, plosives, or single consonants.
5. Greater articulatory breakdown on multisyllabic words than on monosyllabic words.
6. Verbal production of automatic utterances (e.g., counting, listing days of the week) better than the production of novel, volitional utterances.
7. Prosody characterized by flat intonation and inappropriate pauses.
8. Poor oral repetition skills.
9. Intact auditory comprehension skills.
10. Writing skills better than speech skills.
11. Good self-awareness of speech errors.

__. _____
_____
__. _____
_____
__. _____
_____

LONG-TERM GOALS

1. Engage in speech at the conversational level with maximum articulatory accuracy and appropriate prosody.
2. Maintain adequate oral muscular mobility and oral kinesthetic awareness for support of effective articulation.
3. Consistently use compensatory strategies to aid optimal verbal output.
4. Effectively use an adaptive/augmentative communication system to convey needs and wants in the absence of intelligible speech.

—. _____

_____

—. _____

_____

—. _____

_____

SHORT-TERM OBJECTIVES

1. Willingly participate in a comprehensive medical/ neurological assessment. (1)

2. Willingly participate in the speech-language evaluation. (2)

3. Participate with family/ caregiver in a meeting to learn of the evaluation results and agree on an overall intervention strategy. (3)

THERAPEUTIC INTERVENTIONS

1. Confer with the medical team regarding the client's current diagnoses, medical history, previous treatment, and potential for recovery.

2. Administer a complete speech-language evaluation with special emphasis on the oral motor exam, noting especially the client's ability to carry out automatic and volitional oral movements.

3. Arrange an interpretive staffing meeting with the client and caregivers to discuss the findings of the evaluation, the implications of the medical condition for speech, and the prognosis for the recovery of functional communication; obtain information from the

4. Associate the use of volitional movements with symbolic (nonspeech) stimuli. (4)

5. Demonstrate volitional control by carrying out manual gestures with 90% accuracy. (5, 6)

6. Increase mouth opening to improve movement of the oral structures. (7, 8)

family regarding the client's level of education, occupation, and general level of communicative sophistication to design a treatment plan consistent with his/her communicative needs.

4. Instruct the client in the initial stages of Visual Action Therapy (VAT) by asking him/her to finger-trace large pictures of functional objects, providing hand-over-hand assistance if he/she is unable to trace the picture volitionally.

5. Instruct the client in accurate pointing responses when presented with visual stimuli to acquire a sense of volitional control by presenting several pictures and asking him/her to point to the picture requested; extend picture pointing to an open-ended task that requires the client to finish a statement by pointing to a correct picture (e.g., "Walking the ____." The client points to a picture of "dog.") chosen from a field of three or four pictures.

6. Teach the client a group of conventional gestures (e.g., a hand held to the mouth for "Eat" or a C-shaped hand in front of the mouth for "Drink"), modeling the gesture while speaking the word; ask him/her to imitate the gesture without speaking, providing hand-over-hand assistance if he/she is unable to carry out the gesture volitionally.

7. Manually move the client's jaw down until his/her mouth is open as far as possible, then move it

7. Correctly carry out non-speech oral movements with 90% accuracy. (9)

8. Shape nonspeech oral movements into speech movements. (10)

9. Accompany oral movements with the use of manual gestures with 90% accuracy. (11)

10. Physically manipulate the oral structures to facilitate oral movement. (12)

11. Achieve correct articulatory placement in syllables and

back to the closed position; repeat this motion in three sets of five repetitions.

8. Demonstrate slow, exaggerated chewing movements (Chewing Method) to increase the movement and excursion of all the oral structures; ask the client to imitate chewing movements.

9. Model nonspeech oral movements (e.g., smiling, sticking out the tongue, puckering the lips, or biting the lower lip); ask the client to imitate, manually shaping the oral structures into the desired configuration if he/she is unable to do so volitionally.

10. When the client is able to consistently produce nonspeech oral movements, combine the oral movements with sounds (e.g., smile = "eee", biting the lower lip = "fff," puckered lips = "oo"); shape the sounds into simple words (e.g., "eee" into "eeeat" or "fff" into "fffork").

11. Teach the client gestures to accompany speech movements (e.g., opening and closing the hand to indicate opening and closing the mouth or an index finger pointed at each corner of the mouth to indicate "ee").

12. Teach the client to physically manipulate the lips, cheeks, and tongue to facilitate articulatory placement (e.g., holding the lips tightly together to say /p/).

13. Model and elicit imitation of individual sounds and syllables,

words 90% of the time.
(13, 14, 15, 16, 17)

using a mirror to help him/her compare his/her articulatory production to the SLP's.

14. Extend the client's oral production to short meaningful syllables and words such as "Pea" or "Me" using modeling, shadowing, and behavior rehearsal.

15. Encourage the client to say a meaningful syllable or word several times simultaneously with the SLP; gradually reduce the amount of direct imitation by first modeling a word and then mouthing it as he/she says it; model a word once and ask the client to repeat; fade the use of oral modeling by presenting him/her with written or pictorial stimuli and ask him/her to say the target utterance.

16. Locate the context in which the client can most easily produce target sounds, whether at the syllable or word level, and stabilize accurate production of the target sounds at that level; extend correct articulation to the sentence level, using standard articulation exercises, along with modeling and behavior rehearsal.

17. Ask the client questions to elicit correct production of target utterances.

12. Accompany the learning of words and phrases with a manual sign system. (18)

18. Facilitate production of more extended utterances by teaching the client a manual sign system such as Signed English or Amerind, which is used simultaneously with speech.

13. Facilitate the production of multisyllabic words by using rhythmic gestures. (19)

14. Reduce inappropriate pauses using rhythmic speech. (20, 21)

15. Reduce oral struggle behaviors with deep relaxation. (22)

16. Speak using appropriate stress and emphasis patterns 90% of the time. (23, 24, 25)

19. Facilitate the production of multisyllabic words and short phrases by introducing the use of rhythmic gestures (e.g., clapping, tapping, or head-bobbing) for the client to use while he/she speaks.

20. Teach the client to speak along with the beat of a metronome, starting at a rate at which the client can speak without hesitating; gradually increase the rate of the metronome to a level appropriate for him/her, then fade the use of the metronome.

21. Initiate Melodic Intonation Therapy (MIT), teaching the client to first tap out the rhythm of a preestablished phrase (e.g., "How are you?") then to combine the rhythm with a hummed melody that approximates the prosodic contour of the target phrase; combine the words of the phrase with the tapped rhythm and the melody, fading the tapping and the melody until the words are spoken alone.

22. Instruct the client in deep muscle relaxation methods (to be implemented before speaking) to enhance verbal control.

23. Carry out contrastive stress drills with the client using a single sentence, changing its meaning by varying the emphasis given to key words (e.g., "**Why**, John?" versus "Why, **John**?"); model ways to increase volume or raise pitch on the emphasized words.

24. Practice interrogative reversals with the client using appropriate emphasis and prosodic contours (e.g., "We are **going**." versus "**Are** we going?").

25. Model the use of increased vocal intensity and pitch for greater emphasis in speaking, or ask the client to mark words to be emphasized in a reading passage and then ask him/her to read, giving appropriate emphasis to the marked words; critique the client for effectiveness of expression.

17. Effectively use an alternative means of communication if speech is unintelligible. (26, 27)

26. Encourage the client to keep a notebook available for writing utterances when speech is unintelligible.

27. Devise an alternative means of communication (e.g., picture board, alphabet board, or artificial voice output system) for the client and instruct him/her in its use if his/her speech remains unintelligible after trial therapy or as a temporary means of communication during therapy until his/her speech becomes intelligible.

18. Transfer the use of intelligible speech to a variety of social situations. (28, 29)

28. Facilitate group sessions with other speech-impaired clients for the practice of conversational speech, reinforcing the use of speech behaviors learned in therapy.

29. Accompany the client to areas away from the therapy room to engage in social conversation with other persons; record the use of new speech behaviors and

continue the practice until
intelligible, effective speech is
generalized.

__. _____   __. _____
    _____   _____
__. _____   __. _____
    _____   _____
__. _____   __. _____
    _____   _____

DIAGNOSTIC SUGGESTIONS:

Axis I: 307.9   Communication Disorder NOS
                 315.31   Expressive Language Disorder
                 315.39   Phonological Disorder

                 _____   _____
                 _____   _____

AUGMENTATIVE/ALTERNATIVE COMMUNICATION (AAC)

BEHAVIORAL DEFINITIONS

1. Inability to communicate orally because of a traumatic event or acute medical condition.
2. Deteriorating speech intelligibility and oral motor function because of a degenerative medical condition.
3. Inability to restore oral communication following an acute medical condition.
4. Failure to ever develop oral communication because of a physical or developmental disability.
5. Inability to communicate effectively using speech alone.
6. Exhibits sufficient receptive language and cognitive skills to effectively use an augmentative/alternative system.

—. _____

_____

—. _____

_____

—. _____

_____

LONG-TERM GOALS

1. Effectively communicate wants and needs using a combination of oral communication and augmentative/alternative systems.
2. Effectively convey wants and needs, in the absence of usable speech, using a combination of augmentative/alternative communicative systems.

3. Family, staff, and caregivers support the client in the maintenance, care, and use of the augmentative/alternative communication system.

—. _____

 _____

—. _____

 _____

—. _____

 _____

SHORT-TERM OBJECTIVES

1. Participate in the receptive-expressive and cognitive language assessment. (1)

2. Participate in the augmentative communication needs assessment. (2, 3, 4)

THERAPEUTIC INTERVENTIONS

1. Assess the client's receptive and cognitive language skills, including his/her alertness, memory, and ability to follow directions; note the extent to which the client is able to use oral communication.

2. Obtain information from the client and his/her caregivers regarding the types of partners with whom the client will be communicating, the settings in which most communication will occur, and the types of messages that the client will most likely use (e.g., "Yes," "No," requests, greeting).

3. With the assistance of the physical therapist, occupational therapist, and rehabilitation engineer, assess the client's motor skills, endurance, and bodily positioning, considering how these factors will affect his/her ability to access and use an augmentative/alternative communication (AAC) system optimally.

4. Considering the client's medical condition (e.g., temporary and improving, static, or deteriorating), determine whether a simple or sophisticated AAC system is most appropriate at the initiation of treatment; as treatment proceeds, assess the client continuously to determine whether the system should be expanded or altered if his/her proficiency increases and his/her communication needs change.

3. Use a call/alert system with 95% effectiveness. (5, 6)

5. Provide the client with a call light or switch-operated buzzer and teach him/her to use it to get the attention of staff and caregivers to make his/her immediate needs known; if the client's motor skills are too limited to use a switch, teach him/her to clap or tap on the wheelchair or bedrails to get the staff's attention.

6. Inservice the client's staff and caregivers in the use of the call/alert system to ensure that they will be able to respond to him/her in a timely manner.

4. Indicate an accurate yes/no response 90% of the time. (7, 8)

7. Teach the client to make a consistent yes/no response, taking into account his/her physical motor limitations (e.g., head-nod = yes, head-shake = no; thumbs up = yes, thumbs down = no; raised eyebrows = yes, eye blink = no).

8. Instruct the client's communication partners and caregivers in the use of the yes/no system, and teach them to obtain information from the client regarding his/her basic needs by

5. Make basic needs known using a system of physical gestures. (9, 10)

6. Communicate using a standardized manual signing system. (11)

7. Effectively use a written system to communicate needs and wants. (12, 13)

8. Demonstrate 90% accurate visual scanning skills used to spell words necessary for basic communication. (14)

using a series of yes/no questions.

9. With the assistance of the client and his/her communication partners, agree on a set of needs that he/she believes to be the most important to communicate (e.g., "Eat" or "Get me up").

10. Teach the client a gesture to indicate each need (e.g., pointing to the mouth = "Eat," hand held with the palm up = "Get me up").

11. Teach the client to use a limited number of signs from a standardized system (e.g., Signed English) to communicate basic messages; provide staff and communication partners with a manual of the signs, so they will be able to interpret his/her messages.

12. If the client has good cognitive skills and good hand control, provide him/her with a notebook and pen to write out messages.

13. If the client's hand control is limited, consult with the occupational therapist on the use of adaptive equipment to facilitate the client's writing (e.g., pen grips, erasable slates, and lap trays).

14. If the client is unable to use his/her arms, fabricate an alphabet board with the letters arranged in a row-column format, including about five letters in each row; ask the client to think of a message he/she wants to spell out; have the client focus on the first row of

letters, then point to the first row of letters, asking, "Is the first letter you want in this row?"; continue until he/she indicates "Yes" to the target row; move across the row, pointing to each letter, asking, "Is it this letter?" until the client indicates "Yes" on the target letter; continue in this manner until the message is complete.

9. Demonstrate 90% accurate auditory scanning skills used to spell words necessary for basic communication. (15)

15. If the client is visually impaired and unable to focus on an alphabet board, present the letters orally, asking, "Is the first letter A through E?" "Is it F through J?"; continue until he/she indicates "Yes" to the desired group of letters, then name each letter in the group until the desired letter is chosen; continue in this manner until the message is complete.

10. Directly select target messages with 90% accuracy. (16, 17)

16. Teach the client to point directly to target pictures, letters, or words, to communicate a message making adaptations as necessary depending on his/her physical motor limitations; for example, a client with no use of his/her arms may be taught to point with his/her big toe or with a pointer attached to a headband.

17. Fabricate a board with words or pictures important for the client's daily routine; ask him/her to select the target messages using direct eye-gaze; confirm his/her message by stating it orally (e.g., if the client eye-gazes at a picture of a bed, say in response, "You want to go to bed") and waiting for

the client to indicate "Yes" or "No."

11. Operate an adaptive switch with 90% accuracy. (18, 19)

18. Assess the client's ability to use various switches; select the switch that he/she can most easily use given his/her physical motor limitations (e.g., head switches, foot switches, or pneumatic switches to access an electronic communication system may be considered).

19. Model the method of activating the switch to access an electronic communication system for the client; ask him/her to imitate and then use the switch to turn the electronic system on and off.

12. Demonstrate accurate message selection on an electronic communication system using an adaptive switch. (20, 21)

20. Program an electronic system with rows of squares in which each square has a message important to the client; format the system with a horizontal scanning cursor which moves and pauses briefly on each square; ask him/her to select a message he/she wants to communicate; next, ask him/her to activate the switch to start the cursor scanning; cue him/her to activate the switch when the cursor reaches the desired message; wait for the system to deliver the message.

21. Instruct the staff and communication partners in methods of switch activation and message selection to ensure the client's carryover of these skills into activities of daily living.

13. Demonstrate effective use of a print output system. (22, 23)

22. Instruct the client with good direct selection skills in the use

of a system that produces messages in a printed format; depending on the type of system used, instruct the client in the use of features such as word completion and abbreviation expansion to reduce the number of keystrokes needed to write a message and, thereby, deliver the message more quickly.

23. Encourage the client to prepare and store important messages in advance (e.g., questions for the doctor), so they can be printed out quickly when they are needed.

14. Demonstrate effective use of an electronic voice output system. (24, 25)

24. Using a digitized voice output system, record messages into the system that the client wants to communicate which he/she can access using a direct selection or scanning format; change or expand the recorded messages to meet his/her changing communication needs.

25. Using a synthetic voice output system, select a voice quality (e.g., man, woman, or child) that the client prefers; program words, phrases, and sentences that he/she can access for communication using a direct selection or scanning format.

15. Communicate effectively using a combination of electronic and nonelectronic communication systems in a variety of everyday settings. (26, 27, 28)

26. Expand the client's systems with messages that cover a variety of thematic categories (e.g., school, shopping, or restaurant), so they may be used in several social settings.

27. Provide the client with a nonelectronic system (e.g., picture board, alphabet board, or

notebook) to use as a backup in
case of an electronic communication system breakdown.

28. Accompany the client on
outings away from the clinic and
encourage him/her to use the
AAC in more natural situations.

—. _____   —. _____
    _____   _____
—. _____   —. _____
    _____   _____
—. _____   —. _____
    _____   _____

DIAGNOSTIC SUGGESTIONS:

Axis I: 307.9   Communication Disorder NOS
                 799.9   Diagnosis Deferred
                 V71.09   No Diagnosis or Condition

                 _____   _____
                 _____   _____

CEREBRAL PALSY

BEHAVIORAL DEFINITIONS

1. Nonprogressive documented injury to the brain during the prenatal or perinatal developmental period.
2. Neuromotor symptoms that vary because of severity, type (spasticity, athetosis, ataxia, or mixed), or place (hemiplegia, diplegia, or quadriplegia).
3. Persistence of primitive reflexes.
4. Delayed developmental milestones.
5. Difficulty with swallowing.
6. Deficits in clarity and prosody of speech.
7. Respiratory and resonance deficits.
8. Listening comprehension deficits (i.e., receptive aphasia).
9. Verbal and written expression deficits (i.e., expressive aphasia).

—. _____
_____

—. _____
_____

—. _____
_____

LONG-TERM GOALS

1. Develop clear and intelligible speech in conversations.
2. Coordinate respiratory and phonatory movements for speech.
3. Use strategies for effective management of swallowing deficits.
4. Use alternative and/or augmentative communication effectively in social/academic situations.

5. Improve receptive and expressive language skills.
6. Develop social interaction skills appropriate for age, dialect, and cultural expectations in various communicative contexts and monitor success.
7. Parents establish realistic expectations for their child's communicative skills and work collaboratively with the speech-language pathologist (SLP) and other professionals to develop effective treatment strategies.

—. _____
   _____

—. _____
   _____

—. _____
   _____

SHORT-TERM OBJECTIVES

1. Participate willingly in a communicative evaluation to determine daily communicative functioning in different contexts. (1, 2, 3)

THERAPEUTIC INTERVENTIONS

1. Document the client's communicative skills by adapting standardized assessments, as necessary, for receptive and expressive language (e.g., *Rosetti Infant-Toddler Language Scale, Preschool Language Scale-IV, Test of Language Development- P3*, or *Oral Written Language Scales*), phonology (e.g., *Goldman-Fristoe Test of Articulation Competence* or *Bankson-Bernthal Test of Phonology*), intelligibility of speech (e.g., *Children's Speech Intelligibility Measure*), and prosody (e.g., *Prosody-Voice Screening Profile*).

2. Document the client's functional speech and language skills by videotaping and analyzing his/her communicative attempts

2. Cooperate with a complete oral-motor examination. (4)

3. Participate willingly in an audiological assessment. (5)

4. Parents and other professionals contribute to the interpretation of evaluation information.(6, 7)

during play and common daily routines or while discussing favorite conversational topics.

3. Evaluate the client's respiratory patterns during speech and at rest looking for evidence of reversed or belly breathing, breath control, hyperextension, and changes in tone and postural stability.

4. Evaluate the client's oral-motor speech functioning by first observing the visible structure of his/her face, lips, teeth, tongue, hard palate, and soft palate and then assess how he/she uses specific structures important for speech and language production (e.g., movement, strength, and closure of the lips; strength, protrusion, retraction, and lateralization of the tongue; and movement of the soft palate and phonation of voiced sounds; see the Robertson Dysarthria Profile in *Working with Dysarthrics* by Robertson and Thomson for a complete checklist).

5. Perform an audiological screening, referring the client to an audiologist for a complete evaluation if results indicate a need for further assessment.

6. Ask the parents and other professionals to contribute information on the client's developmental milestones, medical history, current medical status, educational status, other professional interventions, communicative attempts in different settings, and social and family concerns.

7. Parents seek ongoing trans-disciplinary evaluations of the client from a physiatrist, pediatrician, neurologist, orthopedic surgeon, educational psychologist, teacher, physical therapist, occupational therapist, social worker, audiologist, and other relevant professionals to document the medical, cognitive, educational, health, hearing, daily living, and motor skills important for developing appropriate communicative interventions.

5. Parents and, if appropriate, the client accept the recommendations developed and collaboratively select communicative behavioral goals that improve the client's quality of life and adhere to the family's priorities and cultural values. (8, 9)

8. Conduct regular meetings with the client's parents and other relevant professionals to develop and modify collaborative intervention strategies as the client makes progress.

9. Select specific communicative situations as targets for intervention for the client based on his/her cognitive, linguistic, social, and academic needs.

6. Parents develop realistic expectations for the client and utilize reliable supportive resources for information. (10, 11)

10. Explain to the client's parents, teachers, and other relevant professionals the relationships between cerebral palsy and communication development.

11. Provide helpful references and resources on cerebral palsy for the client's parents (see *Children with Cerebral Palsy* edited by Geralis and the United Cerebral Palsy Organization web site at http://www.ucp.org) and encourage the parents to join a local cerebral palsy support group.

7. Utilize appropriate environmental supports and

12. Explore with the client's parents, physical therapist, and occupa-

strategies, medical interventions, and adaptive equipment that enhance communicative success. (12)

8. Parents implement specific strategies for feeding the client and encouraging oral-motor development. (13, 14)

9. Use two to three strategies for managing dysphagia. (15)

10. Reduce the frequency and quality of drooling saliva. (16, 17, 18)

tional therapist what environmental supports and adaptive equipment are needed to maximize his/her communicative success (e.g., choosing adaptive equipment for optimal sitting and lying positions, communication boards and electronic devices for alternative/ augmentative communication, and adaptive cups, silverware and oral stimulation devices for feeding and oral motor development); facilitate the client's use of these adaptive supports and strategies.

13. In collaboration with the physical therapist, teach the client's parents the best way to position and/or hold the client that optimally reduces his/her muscle tone.

14. Teach the parents to use stimulation exercises (e.g., using a NUK brush to stimulate areas around the inside and outside of the mouth and to alleviate oral tactile defensiveness or lack of sufficient sensitivity in the oral area).

15. Teach the client and parents, if appropriate, various strategies for dysphagia intervention (see the Dysphagia—Children chapter in this *Planner*).

16. Teach the parents how to massage the client's face with different textured cloths to increase his/her facial sensitivity to the wetness caused by drooling.

17. Explain to the parents, with the assistance of the physical

therapist, how to position the client to reduce the effects of his/her lack of muscle tone, which contributes to the lack of saliva control.

18. Strengthen the client's lip closure by instructing him/her to hold a safe object (e.g., a bite block or pacifier) between his/her lips for increasing lengths of time with and without resistance.

11. If nonverbal, communicate by using alternative/ augmentative communication systems with 80% accuracy. (19)

19. Teach the client to use alternative/augmentative communication to interact effectively in everyday situations (see the Augmentative/ Alternative Communication chapter in this *Planner*).

12. Demonstrate posture and respiratory habits necessary for speech production. (20, 21)

20. Teach the client about the respiratory system including how his/her lungs work, speech versus at-rest breathing, and how he/she can breathe more efficiently using abdominal-diaphragmatic breathing with proper trunk alignment.

21. In consultation with a physical therapist, adjust the client's posture to reduce the effects of a lack of muscle tone, then instruct the client first to take a deep breath using his/her abdomen and diaphragm and exhale slowly with a steady stream of air for up to five seconds.

13. Coordinate respiration and phonation in an efficient manner. (22, 23, 24)

22. If the client exhibits eye, jaw, cervical, and/or lumbar hyperextension when voicing, position him/her with hips flexed in at least a 90 degree position along with thoracic

extension with the assistance of a physical therapist; support the back of his/her head with one hand and his/her chin with your other hand while telling the client to look straight ahead and begin voicing.

23. Prompt the client to begin speaking the moment he/she begins an exhalation; while placing your hand on the client's stomach, ask him/her to inhale and then gently cue the client to vocalize as soon as he/she expels air.

24. Ask the client to say /a/ for up to 15 seconds after taking a deep breath using his/her diaphragm; after he/she is successful, ask the client to say fricative sounds (e.g., /s/ and /z/ for up to five seconds).

14. Teach the client's parents to use facial stimulation techniques to strengthen facial muscles. (25, 26, 27)

25. Teach the client's parents to gently stroke his/her facial muscles with ice in a plastic bag for no longer than five seconds; then, immediately after, teach the parents to help the client perform exercises to strengthen his/her facial muscles.

26. Teach the parents to brush the muscles of the client's face that correspond with the strengthening activity (e.g., the lips or the jaw) with a soft paint brush for one minute before engaging in strengthening exercises; if the client is initially hypersensitive to the brushing, gradually increase the time and intensity of the treatment to build up his/her sensitivity.

27. Teach the parents to use pressure, stretching, and resistance techniques on the muscles of both sides of the client's face to strengthen and facilitate coordinated muscle movements.

15. Increase the precision of producing specific speech sounds in phrases with 80% accuracy. (28)

28. Begin working on improving error consonants in the postvocalic position that the client is able say in the prevocalic position first and then work on improving the articulation of those sounds in the medial position of words (see the Phonological Disorders chapter in this *Planner*).

16. Use compensatory strategies for articulating difficult speech sounds. (29, 30, 31)

29. Experiment with alternative placements of the client's tongue for making speech sounds that most closely approximate the standard (e.g., making the /s/ sound with the tongue tip behind the bottom teeth rather than on the alveolar ridge).

30. Slow the client's speech to a rate that does not interfere with intelligibility but will give him/her the time needed to make articulatory adjustments from one syllable to the next.

31. Teach the client acceptable substitutions for difficult speech sounds, which are easier to make and do not greatly detract from his/her speech intelligibility (e.g., saying a /w/ for /l/ and /r/ sounds).

17. Maintain velopharyngeal closure for nonnasal speech sounds with 80% accuracy. (32, 33, 34)

32. Use visual tools (e.g., hand mirrors below the nose or See-Scape™) to help the client monitor his/her nasal emissions

during productions of minimal contrast pairs (e.g., "mama" and "papa" or "mop" and "pop").

33. If the client does not show a gag reflex, use a cotton swab to stimulate his/her gag reflex by slowly and softly stimulating the palatal area from the alveolar ridge to the soft palate.

34. If the client's velophraryngeal incompetence is severe and the client is not benefiting from stimulation and visualization exercises, investigate with the client's parents and physicians the viability of a palatal lift prosthesis to assist him/her with adequate closure.

18. Use appropriate prosody of speech in phrases with falling, rising, and exclamatory inflections. (35, 36, 37)

35. Determine how many syllables the client can efficiently and clearly say in one breath group; help the client learn to use that optimal number of syllables in his/her production of phrases and pauses.

36. Practice contrastive stress drills that ask the client to overemphasize more important parts of a phrase and deemphasize the least important.

37. Video or audio record the client as he/she is verbalizing questions, declaratives, and exclamations; ask the client to make judgments concerning the appropriateness of his/her loudness, pitch, and stress patterns.

19. Improve receptive and expressive language skills. (38)

38. Use age-appropriate interventions for developing expressive and receptive language (see the Language Disorders—Adolescents,

Language Disorders—Children,
or Language Disorders—
Preschoolers chapters in this
Planner).

—. _____   —. _____
    _____   _____
—. _____   —. _____
    _____   _____
—. _____   —. _____
    _____   _____

DIAGNOSTIC SUGGESTIONS:

Axis I: 307.9   Communication Disorder NOS
                799.9   Diagnosis Deferred
                V71.09   No Diagnosis or Condition

                _____   _____
                _____   _____

CLEFT PALATE

BEHAVIORAL DEFINITIONS

1. Cleft of the hard and/or soft palate.
2. Dental malocclusions.
3. Phonological compensations and/or errors.
4. Middle ear infections resulting in conductive hearing loss.
5. Velopharyngeal incompetence.
6. Weak, tense, and/or hoarse voice.
7. Difficulty with sucking, feeding, and swallowing.
8. Receptive and/or expressive language delays.

—. _____
   _____

—. _____
   _____

—. _____
   _____

LONG-TERM GOALS

1. Develop clear and intelligible speech in conversations.
2. Increase strength and consistency of phonation.
3. Reduce hypernasality and/or hyponasality.
4. Develop age-appropriate receptive and expressive language skills.
5. Parents learn strategies for feeding the client.
6. Parents establish realistic expectations for their child's communicative skills and work collaboratively with the speech-language pathologist (SLP) and other professionals to develop effective treatment strategies.

—. _____
  _____
  _____

—. _____
  _____

—. _____
  _____

SHORT-TERM OBJECTIVES

THERAPEUTIC INTERVENTIONS

1. Participate willingly in a language evaluation to determine receptive and expressive language skills in different contexts. (1, 2)

2. Participate willingly in a speech evaluation to determine the adequacy of phonological development. (3, 4, 5, 6)

1. Document the client's expressive and receptive language skills by administering age-appropriate standardized assessments (e.g., Receptive-Expressive Emergent Language Test, 2nd edition; Rosetti Infant-Toddler Language Scale; Preschool Language Scale-IV; Test of Language Development-P3; Clinical Evaluation of Language Fundamentals-3; or Oral and Written Language Scales).

2. Document the client's conversational speech and language skills over time by videotaping during play and common daily routines or while discussing favorite conversational topics and then analyzing his/her connected speech by completing phonetic inventories and language samples.

3. Evaluate the client's phonological skills by documenting pre- and postsurgical sounds in babbling and early speech.

4. Administer and analyze the client's phonological error patterns on age-appropriate standardized assessments that

particularly assess production of pressure consonants (e.g., Bzoch Error Patterns Diagnostic Articulation Tests and the Iowa Pressure Articulation Test by Morris, Rosen, and Netsell).

5. Ask the client to repeat pressure consonant-vowel combinations (e.g., stops, fricatives, and affricates with different vowels) and to sustain the vowels /i/ and /u/ to determine where the nasal emission begins.

6. Evaluating the client's stimulability skills for error sounds by asking him/her to imitate adult models after hearing and seeing cues for placement.

3. Cooperate with an evaluation of structures used in speech production. (7)

7. Evaluate the client's speech production system by first observing the visible structure of his/her face, lips, teeth, tongue, hard palate, and soft palate; assess the movement, strength, and closure of the lips; strength, protrusion, retraction, and lateralization of the tongue; and movement of the soft palate and phonation of voiced sounds.

4. Participate willingly in an evaluation to determine the adequacy of resonance and phonatory skills. (8, 9, 10)

8. Evaluate the physical adequacy of the velopharyngeal mechanism and the larynx by using direct and indirect laryngoscopy.

9. Evaluate the client's velopharyngeal competence by asking the client to repeat words or sentences with specific phonetic contexts to diagnose hypernasality and/or hyponasality; hold a mirror under his/her nose to look for nasal emission and/or

nasal spray and phoneme specific nasal emission.

10. Determine if the client is using appropriate phonation by asking him/her to sustain the /i/, /a/, and /u/ vowels for longer than 10 seconds; document the presence of aspiration or hoarseness of the voice during this test.

5. Parents and other professionals contribute to the interpretation of evaluation information. (11, 12)

11. Ask the parents and other professionals to contribute information on the client's developmental milestones, medical history and his/her current medical status, educational status, other professional interventions, communication ability in different settings, and social and family concerns.

12. Parents seek ongoing transdisciplinary evaluations from a cleft palate team (e.g., a pediatrician, plastic-reconstructive surgeon, oral-maxillofacial surgeon, orthodontist, pediatric dentist, otolaryngologist, speech-language pathologist, clinical psychologist, social worker, clinical psychologist, audiologist, and teachers) to assist in the development of appropriate communicative interventions.

6. Parents and, if appropriate, the client accept the recommendations developed and collaboratively select communicative behavioral goals. (13, 14)

13. Conduct regular meetings with the client's parents and other relevant professionals to develop and modify collaborative intervention strategies as he/she makes progress.

14. Select specific communicative situations as targets for intervention for the client based on

7. Parents develop realistic expectations for the client and look for positive and supportive resources. (15, 16)

8. Parents, professional members of the client's cleft palate team, and, if appropriate, the client, collaboratively identify and implement appropriate environmental supports and adaptive equipment to enhance communicative success. (17)

9. Parents learn at least three different strategies for increasing the client's oral sensory awareness and range of motion of oral structures. (18, 19, 20)

his/her age, linguistic, social, and academic needs.

15. Explain to the client's parents, teachers, and other relevant professionals the relationships between cerebral palsy and communication development.

16. Provide helpful references and resources on cerebral palsy for the client's parents (see *A Parent's Guide to Cleft Lip and Palate* by Moller, Starr, and Johnson, the Cleft Palate Foundation at http://www.cleftline.org or Wide Smiles at http://www.widesmiles.org); encourage the parents to join a local support group.

17. Explore with the client's parents and the cleft palate team what environmental supports, in addition to surgical interventions, such as pharyngeal flaps, are needed to maximize his/her communicative success (e.g., adaptive nipples and cups or oral stimulation devices for feeding and oral motor development, a palatal lift or obturator for improving velopharyngeal competence).

18. Encourage the parents to provide a variety of safe teething toys for the client to put in his/her mouth.

19. Teach the client's parents to stimulate his/her lips by stroking with a soft brush with firm pressure, rubbing his/her lips with Vaseline, or painting the lips with lip gloss.

10. Parents learn at least three different strategies for stimulating speech and language development during the client's first year. (21)

11. Use two to three strategies appropriate for managing dysphagia. (22)

12. Eliminate glottal stop and pharyngeal fricative substitutions. (23, 24, 25)

13. Achieve velopharyngeal closure and resultant oral

20. Teach the parents to stimulate the client's tongue and alveolar ridge by asking them to brush the ridge and tongue with a toothbrush or place acceptable sticky foods (e.g., jam, cereal, or peanut butter) on the ridge or lips for him/her to lick.

21. Teach the parents to engage in reciprocal babbling play with the client by encouraging oral sounds he/she is able to make (e.g., "baba," "mama," or "nana"); do not encourage or reinforce glottal and pharyngeal sounds (for more strategies, see the Infants-at-Risk chapter in this *Planner*).

22. Teach the client and parents, if appropriate, strategies for dysphagia intervention (see the Dysphagia—Children chapter in this *Planner* for specific swallowing interventions).

23. Teach the client to use the correct articulatory placements for the sounds with tactile, auditory, and visual cues, in contrast to placements for glottal stops and pharyngeal fricatives.

24. Use Speech Viewer (by ProEd) to help the client visualize the differences in productions of glottal stops and pharyngeal fricatives from stops and oral fricatives.

25. Teach the client to say /h/ before beginning the articulatory placement for the voiceless stops, /p/, /t/, and /k/.

26. Use visual tools (e.g., See-Scape™ or a nasometer or

airflow for nonnasal speech sounds with 80% accuracy. (26, 27, 28)

biofeedback techniques) to help the client monitor his/her oral and nasal productions of sounds.

27. Place a straw in the center of the client's front teeth and ask him/her to direct air through the straw as in the /s/ sound.

28. If the client's velopharyngeal incompetence is severe and he/she continues to present nasal emission and hypernasality after establishing oral airflow, investigate the viability of surgical intervention or prosthetics with his/her parents and the cleft palate team to assist with adequate closure.

14. Strengthen the production of affricates, fricatives, and plosive sounds. (29, 30)

29. Begin working on the placements for voiceless stops, fricatives, and affricates to avoid the client's use of compensatory glottal and pharyngeal substitutions.

30. Use visual and tactile cues to encourage the oral airflow necessary for stops, fricatives, and affricates (e.g., gently blowing lightweight mobiles or paper paddles) (see the Phonological Disorders chapter in this *Planner*).

15. Reduce the error pattern of backing with 80% accuracy. (31, 32)

31. Use flavored tongue blades or cotton swabs dipped in juice to contrast placements for front and back sounds; ask the client to place his/her tongue and/or lips in the areas touched and then imitate front and back sounds.

32. Provide practice on minimal contrast paired words (e.g.,

"ra<u>ng</u>" and "ra<u>n</u>" or "<u>c</u>ot" and "<u>t</u>ot") that target the client's habit of backing by asking him/her to request certain pictures or objects or to retell stories using contrasting words with sounds in the back and front tongue positions.

16. Eliminate lateral lisping of the /s/ and /z/ sounds. (33, 34, 35)

33. Consult with the client's dentist and orthodontist to determine if his/her dentition is preventing midline airflow before beginning intervention.

34. If the client can produce a clear /th/ sound, instruct him/her to start with that sound and then slowly retract his/her tongue, placing it on the alveolar ridge or, alternatively, behind his/her lower teeth to produce a non-lateralized /s/; use the /th/ to produce the /z/.

35. If the client can produce a clear /t/, instruct him or her to make a series of rapid, lightly tapped little t-t-t-t-t-ts, which, if said quickly and lightly enough, will become an /s/ with central airflow.

17. Reduce hyponasality of voice. (36, 37, 38)

36. Consult with his/her otolaryngologist to document possible physical blockage of the nasal passages.

37. Teach the client to blow his/her nose by first closing his/her lips and then blowing enough air out of his/her nose to move a paper or tissue in front of the nose; ask the parents to help him/her with this exercise at least two or three times per day.

38. Practice on nasal and nonnasal minimal pairs (e.g., "man" and "ban," "mom" and "bomb," "not" and "dot," "no" and "doe") by using a variety of simple games (e.g., Memory or Go Fish).

18. Reduce phonatory breaks and hoarseness. (39)

39. Use computer-assisted programs (e.g., VisiPitch or Speech Viewer by ProEd) that graphically show changes in pitch to help the client make appropriate changes to his/her habitual pitch level (see strategies for improving voice quality in the Voice Disorders chapter of this *Planner*).

19. Improve receptive and/or expressive language skills. (40)

40. Use age-appropriate interventions for developing expressive and receptive language (see the Language Disorders—Adolescents, Language Disorders—Children, or Language Disorders— Preschoolers chapters in this *Planner*).

__. _____   __. _____
   _____   _____
__. _____   __. _____
   _____   _____
__. _____   __. _____
   _____   _____

DIAGNOSTIC SUGGESTIONS:

Axis I: 307.9   Communication Disorder NOS
              799.9   Diagnosis Deferred
              V71.09   No Diagnosis
              _____   _____
              _____   _____

DEVELOPMENTAL APRAXIA
OF SPEECH

BEHAVIORAL DEFINITIONS

1. During early stages of language acquisition, demonstrates difficulty with purposeful voluntary movements for speech in the absence of paralysis or weakness of the muscles for speech.
2. Difficulty with planning and performing sequential movements for speech.
3. Overall phonological production is substantially below expected developmental norms.
4. Gropes for articulatory positions.
5. Deficit in the awareness of phonological linguistic features, which, in turn, negatively affects speech production.
6. Delays in expressive language development.
7. Disturbances in prosody of speech.
8. Speech production difficulty interferes significantly with effective communication at home, school, and in the community.

__. _____
   _____
__. _____
   _____
__. _____
   _____

LONG-TERM GOALS

1. Improve the planning and production of sequential movements necessary for speech.

2. Maintain intelligibility when communicating with others at home, school, and in the community.
3. Improve prosody of speech in different communicative contexts.
4. Develop understanding of the phonological features of language.
5. Use augmentative/alternative communication effectively in routine communicative situations.
6. Parents establish realistic expectations for their child's phonological development and work collaboratively with the speech-language pathologist (SLP) to develop effective treatment strategies.

—. _____

_____

—. _____

_____

—. _____

_____

SHORT-TERM OBJECTIVES

1. Participate willingly in a phonological assessment. (1, 2, 3, 4)

THERAPEUTIC INTERVENTIONS

1. Administer an articulation test to determine the client's phoneme production in words and in connected speech to assess his/her stimulability for error phonemes and compare his/her phonological development to dialect and developmental norms.

2. Administer a phonological processes test to evaluate the client's error patterns such as final-consonant deletion, initial-consonant deletion, cluster simplification, velar fronting, gliding, depalatization, deaffrication, or fronting.

3. Administer age-appropriate receptive and expressive language tests to establish a measurable baseline of the

client's overall language performance.

4. Videotape a conversational speech sample that represents the client's typical connected speech production while playing with interactive toys or discussing favorite television shows, movies, books or games; analyze the tape for his/her phonological production, amount of verbal production, groping or struggle behaviors, fluency, resonance and voicing characteristics, and expressive language.

2. Cooperate with an oral-motor examination. (5)

5. Evaluate the client's motor skills by first observing his/her overall posture and gait, the visible structure of his/her face, lips, teeth, tongue, hard palate, and soft palate and then assess how he/she uses specific structures important for speech production (e.g., movement, strength, and closure of the lips; strength, protrusion, retraction and movement of the tongue; diadochokinetic rate, and movement of the soft palate when producing the /a/ phoneme).

3. Participate willingly in an audiological evaluation. (6, 7)

6. Conduct a pure-tone audi-ological screening at 500 Hz, 1000 Hz, 2000 Hz, and 4000 Hz at 20 dB for children and 25 dB for adults.

7. Refer the client to an audiologist for a complete evaluation if results of the audiological screening indicate a need for further assessment.

4. Parents participate in the evaluation process and contribute to the interpretation of evaluation information. (8, 9)

5. Parents and the client, if appropriate, accept the recommendations given and collaboratively select intervention goals and a general intervention strategy. (10, 11, 12)

6. Parents accept their child's speech and language deficits relative to the developmental and physical status of their child, develop realistic

8. Ask the parents to provide information on the client's developmental milestones, current medical status and history, previous professional intervention, communication in the home, and relevant social and family concerns.

9. Encourage the parents to seek evaluations from other professionals (e.g., educational psychologist, occupational therapist, physical therapist and/or neurologist) if the client presents with severe developmental apraxia.

10. Conduct a meeting with the parents and the client, if age appropriate, first, to determine his/her eligibility for services and, second, to develop collaborative intervention strategies.

11. Determine the most appropriate general therapeutic approach (i.e., linguistic-based and/or motor-based phonological approaches and/or augmentative/alternative communication) for the client's individual needs.

12. Select specific phoneme movement sequences as targets for intervention based on the client's age, stimulability, intelligibility, dialect, and/or social and educational communicative needs.

13. Explain to the parents the relationships among developmental apraxia and age, language development, and physical status.

expectations, and look for positive and supportive resources. (13, 14, 15)

14. Provide helpful references and resources on developmental apraxia for the parents (see Internet resources from the American Speech-Language-Hearing Association at http://www.asha.org and The Childhood Apraxia of Speech Association at http://www.apraxia-kids.org).

15. Introduce the client's parents to other parents of children with developmental apraxia for informal support or for facilitating their participation in a local support group.

7. Verbalize an understanding of how specific therapeutic interventions contribute to improved phonological skills and how these skills ultimately lead to effective communication. (16, 17, 18)

16. Before beginning intervention, have the client help establish goals and choose stimuli, if age appropriate.

17. Help the client chart therapeutic progress by indicating accomplishments on a visual aid that illustrates the sequential stages necessary for achieving long-term goals.

18. Maintain ongoing, frequent contact with the parents and the client; discuss specific methods for eliciting phonological productions and report progress or concerns regarding the client's phonological needs.

8. Learn to imitate speech sound sequences. (19, 20)

19. Using a mirror large enough to view your face and the client's face, encourage the client to play copy-cat games by first making silly faces together, then making sounds that are relatively easy for the client to make, and, finally, working on more difficult

speech production movement sequences.

20. Praise the client generously when he/she independently looks at your face and attempts to imitate your speech productions.

9. Make the correct articulatory placement for target phonemes. (21, 22, 23, 24)

21. At the beginning of each session, ask the client to do three to five minutes of tongue movement warm-ups by producing the contrasting vowels /i/, /a/, and /u/; sing the vowels to the music and rhythm of the client's favorite songs to encourage playful sound productions.

22. Use mirrors; flavored tongue blades or cotton swab sticks; sticky foods, such as peanut butter; pictures; diagrams; or computer simulations to provide detailed kinesthetic and visual cues to position the client's lips, teeth, and/or tongue for target phonemes.

23. Use programs that use structured tactile cuing, such as Prompts for Restructuring Oral Muscular Phonetic Targets (PROMPT) by Chumpelik or the Touch-Cue program by Bashir, Graham-jones, and Bostwick to practice sequential speech movements.

24. Use phonemes with similar distinctive features to elicit target phonemes (e.g., ask the client to repeat the aspirated /t/ phoneme quickly to produce the /s/ phoneme); point out that the articulator positions are similar.

10. Increase the accuracy of consonant-vowel and vowel-consonant productions by 80% as judged by the SLP. (25, 26, 27)

25. Use a computer program, such as SpeechViewer III by IBM, to provide auditory and graphic speech models for the client to match; begin with syllables with contrasting vowels /i/, /a/, and /u/ in combination with consonants that the client can say; once these combinations are mastered, begin working on productions with other phonemes.

26. Write different consonant-vowel combinations (e.g., CV, VC, VCV) using consistent color codes for the vowels as visual cues for the client to use for practicing sequential movements; combine with picture cues if the client is preliterate.

27. Ask the client to practice consonant-vowel combinations with his/her parents that include increasingly difficult coarticulatory positions for five to ten minutes per day to increase the client's range of tongue movement.

11. Discriminate correctly between contrasting phonological features with 90% accuracy. (28, 29, 30)

28. Use pictures of minimal pair words that contrast phonological features, such as open and closed syllables (e.g., "me" and "meet," "shy" and "shine," or "bow" and "bone"); say the words for the client by overemphasizing the contrasting phonological features and then sort the pictures into the contrasting categories for the client.

29. Teach the client to sort contrasting word cards into two categories of phonological

features independently after listening to models of each word.

30. Use a structured auditory discrimination program, such as the Lindamood Phonemic Sequencing™ (LiPS™) Program, to increase the client's phonemic awareness.

12. Learn to self-monitor accurate speech productions. (31, 32, 33)

31. Ask the client to judge the accuracy of his/her speech attempts immediately after he/she produces the target; instruct him/her to keep track by using visual feedback systems, such as dropping blocks in a can, coloring smiley faces, or using thumbs-up, to indicate good productions.

32. Say the client's incorrect patterns of speech production purposefully on some words and instruct him/her to listen carefully and say, "I heard it!" after hearing the incorrect production.

33. While viewing video recordings of the client practicing intervention strategies, ask the client to identify his/her best productions and those that need improvement.

13. Pronounce target phoneme combinations correctly in words with 90% accuracy. (34)

34. Instruct the client to choose and say one of the minimal contrasting paired words (e.g., "see" and "seat" or "key" and "tea") that target the client's phonological processes; point to the picture that represents what the client actually said (e.g., if the client meant to say "key" and actually said "tea," point to "tea"); dis-

14. Pronounce target phonemes correctly in phrases and sentences with 80% accuracy. (35)

15. If nonverbal, communicate by using augmentative/ alternative communication systems during daily routines with 80% accuracy. (36)

16. Use fluent speech in different conversational situations. (37)

cuss how saying different sounds influences the meaning of what we say.

35. See the Phonological Disorders chapter in this *Planner* for interventions to improve phoneme productions at the phrase and sentence levels.

36. Teach the client to use augmentative/alternative communication to interact effectively in everyday situations (see Augmentative/ Alternative Communication chapter in this *Planner* for specific interventions).

37. First, determine if the client's dysfluent behaviors are related to articulatory difficulty or if they are a separate issue; if related, work on phonological goals; if a separate issue, see Fluency Disorders in this *Planner* for specific interventions.

__. _____
     _____
__. _____
     _____
__. _____
     _____

__. _____
     _____
__. _____
     _____
__. _____
     _____

DIAGNOSTIC SUGGESTIONS:

Axis I: 307.9   Communication Disorder NOS
                 315.31   Expressive Language Disorder
                 315.39   Phonological Disorder

                 _____   _____
                 _____   _____

DYSARTHRIA

BEHAVIORAL DEFINITIONS

1. Slurred, mushy sounding speech because of weak and imprecise articulation.
2. Distorted production of vowels.
3. Consistently breathy voice.
4. Excessively harsh or strained voice.
5. Tremulous voice.
6. Monotone voice.
7. Irregular fluctuations of vocal intensity.
8. Vocal pitch abnormally high or low for the age or gender of the speaker.
9. Lack of appropriate stress and emphasis patterns in connected speech.
10. Short rushes of speech followed by long pauses.
11. Loud, breathy inhalation.
12. Weak inhalation and exhalation.
13. Excessive nasal resonance sometimes accompanied by nasal emissions.

__. _____
    _____
    _____
__. _____
    _____
    _____
__. _____
    _____

LONG-TERM GOALS

1. Maintain optimal respiration for the support of speech.
2. Engage in speech at the conversational level using functional phonation, balanced resonance, and appropriate prosody.

3. Maintain adequate oral-muscular strength and mobility for the support of effective articulation.
4. Engage in speech at the conversational level with maximum articulatory accuracy.
5. Effectively use an augmentative/adaptive communication system to convey needs and wants in the absence of intelligible speech.

—. _____
   _____

—. _____
   _____

—. _____
   _____

SHORT-TERM OBJECTIVES

1. Participate in a comprehensive medical/ neurological assessment. (1)

2. Participate in the speech-language evaluation. (2)

3. Participate with family/ caregiver in a meeting to learn of the evaluation results and agree on an overall intervention strategy. (3)

THERAPEUTIC INTERVENTIONS

1. Confer with the medical team on the client's current diagnosis, medical history, previous treatment, and potential for recovery.

2. Administer the speech-language evaluation focusing on oral motor strength and mobility, articulation, phonation, prosody, and respiration; assess the amount of postural and muscular support needed to compensate for muscular weakness.

3. Arrange an interpretive staffing meeting with the client and caregivers to discuss the findings of the evaluation, the implications of the medical condition for speech, and the prognosis for recovery of functional communication; obtain information from the family regarding the client's occupation and level of

education and communicative sophistication to design a treatment plan consistent with his/her communicative needs.

4. Achieve the necessary physical support of the torso in a manner that will allow optimal respiration. (4)

4. Confer with the client's physician and physical therapist on the safest and most effective method for positioning the client in his/her chair or wheelchair, using adaptive cushions, wedges, corsets, and braces that will provide optimal support for respiration.

5. Use correct abdominal-diaphragmatic breathing patterns. (5, 6)

5. Place hands on the client's abdomen and apply pressure while asking him/her to inhale, hold, and exhale; repeat up to 10 times.

6. Ask the client to inhale and exhale sharply in short bursts, phonating /a/, /a/, /a/, while holding his/her mouth open wide; practice five sets of three repetitions.

6. Increase vocal fold adduction to reduce breathy vocal quality. (7, 8)

7. Ask the client to place his/her hands against a table, lean forward, and then push away from the table while sharply phonating /a/; repeat 10 times.

8. Model hard glottal attack on initial vowels of syllables and words; ask the client to imitate and extend the use of hard glottal attack into phrases and sentences.

7. Decrease laryngeal tension to reduce harsh, strained vocal quality. (9)

9. Model breathy phonatory onset on initial vowels of syllables and words; ask the client to imitate and practice breathy onset using a prolonged initial /h/ phoneme in words, phrases, and sentences, eventually fading

the prolonged /h/ to one of normal duration.

8. Increase velar strength and mobility for velopharyngeal closure. (10, 11, 12)

10. Teach the patient to impound air in the oral cavity by tightly holding his/her lips together and asking him/her to blow up his cheeks while feeling the velum touching the rear wall of the pharynx.

11. Ask the client to say lists of syllables and words with prolonged initial /k/ and /g/ phonemes to facilitate posterior velar movement.

12. Confirm that velopharyngeal (VP) closure is achieved by asking the client to hold his/her hand under the nostrils while blowing up his/her cheeks; if VP closure is adequate, no air will be felt escaping from the nostrils.

9. Reduce excessive nasal resonance. (13)

13. Ask the client to read short passages that contain no nasal phonemes; ask him/her to judge the quality of the reading by marking each syllable or word in which he/she hears nasality.

10. Increase the strength and contact of the lips for accurate articulation of lip placement phonemes. (14, 15)

14. Teach the client lip strengthening exercises, including pucker-release and smile-release; carry out three sets of 10 repetitions each.

15. Increase the strength of lip approximation by asking the client to tightly close his/her lips around a tongue depressor and hold it for up to 10 seconds; repeat up to 10 times.

11. Increase the strength and mobility of the tongue for accurate articulation of

16. Instruct the client in tongue strengthening and range of motion exercises including

tongue placement phonemes. (16)

12. Increase mouth opening to improve movement of the oral structures. (17, 18, 19)

13. Physically support the oral structures to compensate for oral muscular weakness. (20)

14. Achieve correct articulatory placement in syllables and words. (21, 22, 23)

tongue protrusion-retraction, elevation-depression, and lateralization; practice each exercise in three sets of 10 repetitions.

17. Manually move the client's jaw down until his/her mouth is open as far as possible, then move it back to the closed position; repeat this motion in three sets of five repetitions; ask him/her to initiate this movement without manual assistance.

18. After the client demonstrates effective mouth opening and closing, ask him/her to say repetitive syllables (e.g., /ma-ma-ma/, /ja-ja-ja/, /da-da-da/) in an exaggerated manner.

19. Demonstrate slow, exaggerated chewing movements (Chewing Method) to increase the movement and excursion of all the oral structures; ask the client to imitate the chewing movements while phonating /a/ at the same time.

20. Teach the client to manually support the lips and/or cheeks to facilitate articulatory placement (e.g., tightly holding the lips together to say /p/); fade the manual support, if possible.

21. Model individual phonemes for the client; ask the client to imitate.

22. When client is able to imitate accurate articulatory placement, engage in modeling and behavior rehearsal of exaggerated articulatory contact (overarticulation).

15. Correctly articulate target phonemes up to the sentence level. (24)

16. Speak using appropriate stress and emphasis patterns. (25)

17. Speak at a rate within the normal range. (26, 27)

18. Effectively use an augmentative or alternative means of communication if speech is unintelligible. (28, 29)

23. Engage in modeling and behavior rehearsal of contrastive pairs (e.g., "sew-tow" or "pay-bay") using exaggerated articulatory contact.

24. Locate the context in which the client can most easily produce target phonemes, whether it is at the syllable or word level, and stabilize accurate production of the target phonemes at that level; using standard articulation exercises along with modeling and behavior rehearsal, extend correct articulation to the sentence level.

25. Carry out contrastive stress drills using a single sentence, changing its meaning by varying the emphasis given to key words (e.g., "**Why**, John?" versus "Why **John?**"); model ways to increase volume or raise pitch on the emphasized words.

26. Set a metronome at a rate comfortable for the client, and ask him/her to say a syllable or word on each beat; gradually increase or decrease the rate until it approximates normal speech; fade use of the metronome.

27. Using a pacing board, ask the client to tap on each space of the board with his/her hand or index finger while accompanying each tap with a spoken syllable or word; gradually fade use of the pacing board.

28. Coach the client in the use of a small microphone and amplifier set to increase his/her volume when speaking.

19. Transfer the use of intelligible speech to a variety of social situations. (30)

29. Devise an alternative means of communication (e.g., a picture board, an alphabet board, or writing on a notepad) for the client and instruct him/her in its use if his/her speech remains unintelligible after trial therapy or as a temporary mode of communication during therapy until his/her speech becomes intelligible.

30. Role-play functional scenarios with the client, reinforcing the use of the speech behaviors learned in therapy; accompany the client to areas away from the therapy room (e.g., the dining room, classroom, or activity room) and record the extent to which the new speech behaviors are used, continuing such practice until intelligible, effective communication is generalized.

—. _____
   _____

—. _____
   _____

—. _____
   _____

—. _____
   _____

—. _____
   _____

—. _____
   _____

DIAGNOSTIC SUGGESTIONS:

Axis I: 307.9   Communication Disorder NOS

_____   _____

_____   _____

DYSPHAGIA—ADULT

BEHAVIORAL DEFINITIONS

1. Excessive drooling.
2. Spillage of food or liquid from the mouth when eating.
3. Prolonged time chewing food.
4. Swallowing large pieces of food without chewing.
5. Taking more than one swallow per bite of food or sip of liquid.
6. Holding food in the mouth without swallowing.
7. Pocketing food in one or both cheeks.
8. Complaints of food sticking in the throat or "going down the wrong pipe."
9. Frequent coughing, sneezing, or eye-tearing while eating.
10. Significant weight loss without other medical conditions that would account for the weight loss.
11. Recurring fever without other medical conditions that would account for fever.
12. Recurring pneumonia.
13. Aspiration directly observed during radiographic evaluation.

__. _____
   _____
__. _____
   _____
__. _____
   _____

LONG-TERM GOALS

1. Oral intake of the least restrictive diet to meet the client's nutritional needs without aspiration.
2. Oral feeding supplemented with nonoral feeding to ensure adequate nutritional intake.
3. Maintain adequate nutrition primarily using nonoral feeding supplemented with small oral feedings for pleasure.
4. Maintain adequate nutrition using nonoral feedings only.

__. _____
   _____
   _____

__. _____
   _____
   _____

__. _____
   _____

SHORT-TERM OBJECTIVES

1. Provide medical history and current level of functioning relevant to eating, swallowing, general nutritional status, and food preferences. (1, 2)

2. Cooperate with a thorough swallow evaluation. (3, 4)

THERAPEUTIC INTERVENTIONS

1. Obtain relevant medical background from the client or family, including history of stroke, neurological impairment, and dental status (e.g., Does the client use dentures, partials, or is he/she accustomed to eating without teeth?), and cognitive status.

2. Obtain information on the client's food preferences and eating habits, designing the plan of treatment to accommodate these preferences.

3. Perform an oral-motor exam and bedside swallow evaluation, assessing the oral and pharyngeal phases of the swallow; trial differing quantities and consistencies of food.

3. Accept the SLP's recommendations for treatment and the type of nutritional intake and food consistency, while participating in setting realistic expectations for treatment. (5)

4. Increase the strength of the lips and cheeks to 90% for adequate retention and manipulation of food in the oral cavity. (6)

5. Hold food and liquid in the mouth without spillage from the lips 90% of the time. (7, 8)

6. Masticate food sufficiently within 10 seconds per mouthful. (9, 10, 11)

4. If aspiration of food or liquid is suspected, arrange a videofluoroscopic swallow evaluation for the client by obtaining the necessary medical referrals.

5. On receiving the clinical report of the videofluoroscopy, discuss with the client and/or family the findings of the evaluation, its significance for treatment, and the client's prognosis; recommend for him/her the least restrictive diet for the most effective nutritional intake, as well as an appropriate level of supervision for feeding him/her; agree on a plan of treatment.

6. Increase the strength and approximation of the client's lips by assigning him/her to hold a tongue depressor between the lips for up to five seconds; repeat five to ten times.

7. Strengthen the client's lips for improved closure by having him/her pucker-release and smile-release the lips; carry out three sets of 10 repetitions each.

8. Directly assist the client in achieving lip closure by manually supporting his/her jaw or holding the lips closed when eating.

9. To increase jaw movement for mastication, ask the client to open his/her mouth as wide as possible and then close and then ask him/her to move the jaw from side to side; apply manual resistive pressure to the jaw as the client carries out the

movements; carry out three sets of 10 repetitions each.

10. If the client is unable to achieve effective jaw movement, instruct him/her to use the tongue to mash soft foods against the hard palate.

11. Place food on the stronger side of the client's mouth or tilt his/her head to the stronger side to improve mastication.

7. Use coordinated tongue movements to manipulate food into a cohesive bolus. (12, 13, 14)

12. Instruct the client in tongue strengthening and range of motion exercises to facilitate bolus manipulation, including tongue protrusion-retraction, elevation-depression, and lateralization; introduce resistance by having him/her push the tongue against a tongue depressor; practice each exercise in three sets of 10 repetitions.

13. Using a narrow piece of cloth or gauze, ask the client to hold one end of the gauze in his/her mouth between the tongue and hard palate while the SLP holds the other end; ask him/her to move the gauze forward and backward and from side to side.

14. Place a small amount of puree or pudding-consistency food on the client's tongue and then ask him/her to move the material against the hard palate without letting the food dissipate in the mouth; if he/she is "Nothing Per Oral," remove the food using a finger sweep or by instructing him/her to expectorate it.

8. Propel the bolus, using coordinated tongue

15. Teach the client to move the tongue from the alveolar ridge

movements, to the rear of the oral cavity with 90% accuracy. (15, 16)

back to the soft palate while maintaining the tongue's contact with the palate throughout.

16. Facilitate bolus propulsion by lubricating the client's oral cavity with a small sip of liquid before presenting the solid food; present food that forms a cohesive bolus that will easily move back in the oral cavity.

9. Initiate the swallow reflex within one to two seconds. (17, 18)

17. Perform thermal stimulation to increase sensitivity at the rear of the oral cavity by using a small laryngeal mirror or metal probe dipped in ice water and then applied to the base of the faucial pillars; after application of the probe to the faucial pillars, instruct the client to swallow; repeat up to 10 times.

18. After thermal stimulation, present the client with a small amount of liquid that he/she will swallow on command; gradually increase the thickness and texture of the boluses to be swallowed within one to two seconds.

10. Avoid premature spillage of the food or liquid from the oral cavity into the pharyngeal cavities. (19, 20)

19. Facilitate base of tongue elevation to increase contact of the tongue with the pharyngeal wall, via modeling and behavior rehearsal of isolated /k/ sounds and words with initial /k/ (e.g., "cake," "cookie"); hold each initial /k/ for one second and release it sharply.

20. Instruct the client in the chin tuck technique by asking him/her to tilt his/her head forward, bringing the chin close to the chest, and then swallowing;

11. Achieve consistent glottal closure when swallowing to prevent food from entering the trachea. (21, 22)

12. Increase laryngeal elevation to reduce the entrance of food or liquid into the airway and to reduce the accumulation of food in the pharyngeal cavities. (23, 24)

13. Increase pharyngeal strength to reduce the accumulation of food in the pharyngeal cavities. (25, 26)

practice first using dry swallows, then with food or liquid.

21. Increase the strength of the client's glottal closure by instructing him/her to forcibly push away from a table while phonating /a/ for up to 10 repetitions.

22. Instruct the client in the Safe Swallow technique following the "take a breath, hold, swallow, cough, swallow again" sequence; practice first using dry swallows, then add food or liquid, ensuring that he/she follows the sequence with each mouthful.

23. Have the client produce a high-pitched /i/ sound for three to five seconds while he/she simultaneously palpates the neck to feel the elevation of the larynx during phonation.

24. Instruct the client in the use of the Mendelsohn Maneuver by asking him/her to volitionally hold the larynx at its highest point in the neck during the swallow while simultaneously palpating the neck to feel the elevation the larynx.

25. Increase the client's pharyngeal strength using the Makasa Maneuver, instructing him/her to hold the tip of the tongue between the upper and lower incisors while swallowing hard at the same time; the client should report feeling a sharp pull in the throat.

26. Instruct the client in Logemann's Effortful Swallow, cueing him/her to "swallow hard";

practice first using dry swallows, then add food or liquid, ensuring that he/she does this with each mouthful.

14. Demonstrate effective oral and pharyngeal management of the least restrictive diet using the compensatory and facilitative strategies learned in treatment. (27, 28, 29)

27. Confer with the facility's dietary personnel in making appropriate recommendations for the least restrictive diet that will ensure safe oral intake for the client.

28. Train the facility's nursing staff on safe feeding procedures to be implemented with the client; recommend a level of meal supervision appropriate to his/her physical condition and cognitive status.

29. After treatment concludes, periodically monitor the client during meal time to ensure that he/she demonstrates effective carryover of the compensatory and facilitative techniques learned in therapy; make revised dietary recommendations, if indicated.

__. _____

_____

__. _____

_____

__. _____

_____

__. _____

_____

__. _____

_____

__. _____

_____

DIAGNOSTIC SUGGESTIONS:

Axis I: 799.9   Diagnosis Deferred
               V71.09   No Diagnosis or Condition

_____   _____

_____   _____

DYSPHAGIA—CHILD

BEHAVIORAL DEFINITIONS

1. Delayed oral-motor skills.
2. Poorly coordinated suck-swallow-breathe pattern when bottle feeding.
3. Weak suck response.
4. Excessive drooling.
5. Coughing or gagging when feeding.
6. Frequent emesis and/or rumination.
7. Slow feeding and fatigue during feeding.
8. Tactile and/or sensory defensiveness in and around the oral cavity.
9. Aversions to certain foods and textures.
10. Preference for liquids over solids.
11. Unexplained weight loss and inability to maintain age-appropriate weight levels.
12. Unexpected change in feeding patterns.
13. Aspiration of food or refluxed material.
14. Long-term feeding via G-tube or NG-tube.

—. _____
   _____
   _____

—. _____
   _____
   _____

—. _____
   _____

LONG-TERM GOALS

1. Develop age-appropriate oral-motor skills.
2. Reduce oral sensory and tactile aversions.

3. Attain an oral intake of food on the least restrictive diet to meet nutritional needs without aspiration.
4. Maintain adequate nutritional intake on an appropriate combination of oral and enteral feeding.

___. _____

_____

___. _____

_____

___. _____

_____

SHORT-TERM OBJECTIVES

1. Cooperate with an oral/ swallowing evaluation. (1, 2, 3)

2. Parents and transdisciplinary professionals accept recommendations and agree on an overall treatment plan. (4, 5)

THERAPEUTIC INTERVENTIONS

1. Obtain pertinent information from the medical team on the client's health status, including current method of nutritional intake, pulmonary status, and level of attention that will affect feeding/swallowing intervention.

2. Perform an oral/feeding evaluation, assessing the strength and mobility of the oral structures, sucking response, mastication (in an older child), tactile and sensory defensiveness, and food or texture aversions.

3. Arrange a videofluoroscopic swallow evaluation to fully assess pharyngeal functioning and to rule out aspiration.

4. On completion of the evaluation, discuss with the family and the multidisciplinary treatment team the assessment findings, their significance for treatment, and prognosis; recommend an appropriate means of nutritional

intake; agree on an intervention plan.

5. Inservice the medical staff on procedures that positively impact the client's oral/feeding status, such as reducing light and noise levels, avoiding overstimulation of the client, weighing the risks and benefits of prolonged use of enteral feeding, and understanding the importance of oral stimulation for the client's oral-motor development.

3. Demonstrate a calm state of attention for feeding readiness. (6, 7, 8)

6. To reduce the arousal level in an overstimulated client, dim bright lights and reduce loud background noise to provide a distraction-free environment.

7. Physically stabilize the client by swaddling him/her or by applying deep pressure to the body; consult with the occupational therapist on what level of pressure is appropriate.

8. Reduce the client's feeling of physical disorganization by handling him/her with slow, deliberate movements.

4. Demonstrate increased alertness for feeding readiness. (9, 10, 11)

9. Promote the attention of the lethargic client by increasing the stimulation level of the immediate environment with bright lights, colorful visual stimuli, and energetic background music.

10. Increase the client's tactile attention by lightly squeezing, tapping, and tickling his/her arms, legs, and trunk.

11. Increase the client's overall physical attention by handling

5. Achieve optimal positioning for feeding. (12)

6. Reduce oral sensitivity to tactile stimulation. (13, 14, 15, 16)

him/her with firm, unpredictable movements.

12. Confer with the physical and occupational therapist on the most stable method of positioning the client for feeding/swallowing intervention, considering his/her age, muscle tone, head and trunk control, and coexisting medical problems.

13. Initiate deep-pressure massage to increase the client's tolerance of being touched; manipulate his/her arms, legs, and trunk, avoiding direct contact with the face or mouth.

14. Initiate tactile contact with the client's face, massaging the jaw and cheek areas and gradually moving to the lips; if he/she shows tension or discomfort, pause until he/she relaxes and then resume the massage.

15. Probe the client's mouth with a gloved finger, applying gentle pressure on the gums and the inside of the cheeks, moving the finger from the front to the back of the mouth.

16. Introduce a tongue depressor or toothette into the client's mouth, stroking the gums, tongue, and cheek cavities; encourage him/her to hold the probe using a hand-over-hand assist; use firm pressure for clients with high muscle tone and light pressure for clients with low tone; withdraw the probe if he/she gags or shows discomfort.

7. Reduce oral sensitivity to temperature. (17)

17. Dip a toothette into chilled water and insert it into the client's

mouth, massaging the gums, cheek cavities, and tongue.

8. Increase tolerance of strong flavors. (18)

18. Dip a toothette or gloved finger into juices of different flavors (e.g., mildly tangy, bitter, or salty) and massage the inside of the client's mouth; increase the intensity of the flavor as he/she demonstrates increased tolerance.

9. Increase oral self-awareness skills. (19, 20)

19. Encourage the client to explore his/her mouth by inserting his/ her fingers into the mouth and moving the fingers around while modeling oral movements.

20. Encourage the client to hold pacifiers and teething rings, providing a hand-over-hand assist if necessary, and to mouth and manipulate them orally; model oral movements as he/she mouths the implements.

10. Improve oral motor skills. (21, 22, 23)

21. Increase lip mobility and closure to hold food in the mouth by manually holding the lips together and massaging around the lips with deep pressure for clients with high muscle tone; use regular, rhythmic tapping around the lips for clients with low muscle tone.

22. Increase tongue strength and mobility for bolus manipulation by stroking the client's tongue from back to front to improve forward-backward movements; stroke the sides of the tongue and manually move it from side to side to promote lateral movements.

23. Improve the tone and mobility of the cheeks to facilitate

sucking, holding food in the mouth, and chewing by firmly stroking the cheeks from below the ears to the chin for client's with high muscle tone; provide gentle, rhythmic tapping to the cheeks for clients with reduced tone.

11. Establish nonnutritive sucking as a prerequisite to oral feeding. (24, 25)

24. Insert a gloved finger into the client's mouth and apply repetitive pressure on the dorsum of the tongue until he/she begins sucking; remove the finger intermittently to note whether he/she continues sucking; if the client stops, reinsert the finger and apply repetitive pressure to the tongue again.

25. Place a pacifier in the client's mouth; as he/she begins to suck, repetitively pull the pacifier to the front of his/her mouth and gently push it back in, promoting lip approximation and forward-backward tongue movement.

12. Transition from nonnutritive sucking to nutritive sucking. (26)

26. When the client has established the nonnutritive suck, introduce bottle feeding, adjusting the nipple size, pliability, and rate of output of the bottle until he/she is able to maintain a suck-swallow-breathe ratio of 1:1:1.

13. Transition feeding from liquids to solids. (27, 28, 29)

27. Present the client with feedings of thickened liquid or liquid-like puree via bottle, adjusting the nipple output to accommodate the increased texture of the food.

28. Place a small amount of puree on the client's lips and encourage him/her to lick the food off the lips; gradually

increase the number of presentations.

29. Place a small amount of puree on the tip of a spoon and encourage the client to lick the food off the spoon; gradually increase the number of presentations.

14. Establish functional mastication skills. (30, 31)

30. Present the client with puree containing a few small chunks of the same food, which can be manipulated easily in the mouth (e.g., pureed pears with small pear chunks); manually move his/her jaw to promote manipulation of the food.

31. Place soft food on the client's molars or on the lateral aspect of the mouth to promote tongue lateralization and jaw movement by manually manipulating the jaw in a rotary motion to encourage chewing movements; gradually increase the presentations of chunky food.

15. Increase the variety and texture of foods eaten. (32, 33)

32. Systematically habituate the client to varying flavors and textures of food by changing one dimension at a time (e.g., if he/she is accustomed to eating applesauce, change the flavor by introducing pureed peaches— maintaining the texture while altering the flavor—or change the texture by introducing soft chunks of apple—altering the texture while maintaining the flavor).

33. Introduce new foods by mixing them with preferred foods and gradually increasing the amount of the new food in the mixture.

16. Demonstrate adequate oral intake on the least restrictive diet using appropriate eating utensils. (34, 35, 36)

34. Confer with the occupational therapist regarding what feeding utensils provide the client with the most efficient oral food intake.

35. Confer with the dietician on the type of diet that would provide the maximum nutritional benefit for the client; recommend the least restrictive consistency for safe, effective oral intake.

36. Instruct the family and facility staff members on the most effective techniques for feeding the client, including proper positioning, food preparation, and safe feeding.

—. _____   —. _____
   _____   _____
—. _____   —. _____
   _____   _____
—. _____   —. _____
   _____   _____

DIAGNOSTIC SUGGESTIONS:

Axis I: 799.9   Diagnosis Deferred
               V71.09   No Diagnosis

               _____   _____
               _____   _____

FLUENCY DISORDERS

BEHAVIORAL DEFINITIONS

1. Repeats individual sounds, syllables, words, or phrases when attempting to communicate.
2. Stuttering occurs in 10% or more of conversational speech.
3. Struggle behaviors (e.g., eye-blinking, grimacing, or muscular tension) accompany stuttering.
4. Excessive, atypical use of interjections (e.g., "Uh," "Um," "Er," "Well") that interrupt the smooth flow of speech.
5. Atypically prolongs the sound of some words.
6. Broken words (e.g., "I was w___ [pause] ___alking away.") interrupt fluency.
7. Engages in word revision (e.g., "I was-I mean-I am walking there") in an attempt to overcome blocking.
8. Circumlocuitous utterances are used to avoid difficult words.
9. Consistently avoids anxiety-producing speaking situations (e.g., talking on the telephone).
10. A family history of stuttering.
11. Speech and language onset was delayed.
12. Family members have had unrealistic expectations and demands of the client's speech development.
13. Labels self as a stutterer.
14. Perceives own manner of speaking as a social or vocational detriment.
15. Engages in rapid, jerky, indistinct utterances with frequent telescoping of words and phrases without associated fear, anticipation, or a sense of difficulty (cluttering).

—. _____
   _____

—. _____
   _____

—. _____

_____

LONG-TERM GOALS

1. Develop conversational speech that is at least 95% fluent.
2. Maintain fluency by consistent use of self-monitoring strategies.
3. Family and significant others promote and reinforce fluent speech in everyday situations.

—. _____

_____

_____

—. _____

_____

_____

—. _____

_____

SHORT-TERM OBJECTIVES

1. Willingly participate in the speech-language evaluation. (1, 2)

2. Identify and analyze the types of stuttering behaviors produced. (3)

THERAPEUTIC INTERVENTIONS

1. Administer a complete speech-language evaluation with special attention given to fluency, assessing the types of dys-fluency, as well as their frequency and severity in reading and conversation; note associated struggle behaviors (e.g., eye-blinking, head and neck tension).

2. If the client is a student, arrange an interpretive staffing or IEP meeting to discuss the findings of the evaluation and to present the intervention program.

3. Discuss the types of dysfluencies with the client that he/she produces (e.g., prolongation of words,

repetition of sounds, words or phrases, use of interjections, use of broken words); model his/her dysfluencies and explain the various behaviors involved in producing the dysfluency.

3. Establish a hierarchy of speaking situations in which stuttering and anxiety occur. (4, 5)

4. Ask the client to describe situations in which he/she stutters excessively (e.g., talking to strangers or talking on the telephone) and little or not at all (e.g., with close friends); ask whether feelings of anxiety or embarrassment accompany the speaking situations.

5. Establish a hierarchy of speaking situations specific to the client, arranging them in order from the least to the most severe stuttering.

4. Reduce anxiety and demonstrate 95% fluency by using relaxation methods. (6, 7, 8, 9)

6. Instruct the client in progressive deep muscle and deep breathing relaxation techniques in which he/she learns to discriminate between states of muscular tension and relaxation.

7. Lead the client in guided imagery exercises, progressively going through a hierarchy of imagined speaking situations from the least to the most difficult; ask him/her to imagine speaking fluently at each level.

8. Role-play situations selected from the client's stress hierarchy, progressively increasing the difficulty, asking him/her to monitor his/her level of relaxation in each situation; achieve at least 95% fluency at each level.

9. Accompany the client in real-life speaking situations outside

the clinic, beginning with situations in which he/she will easily achieve fluency (e.g., talking to friends) and then proceeding to difficult situations (e.g., taking to a store clerk or making a phone call); use reassurance, relaxation prompts, and reinforcement of success.

5. Demonstrate easy phonatory onset 95% of the time using efficient airflow techniques. (10, 11, 12)

10. Teach the client to inhale deeply and exhale slowly, maintaining a relaxed, open airway throughout; repeat several times.

11. Using controlled airflow, ask the client to gently phonate an /a/; repeat several times.

12. Using easy phonatory onset, ask the client to say syllables and words with initial vowels; extend to short phrases.

6. Demonstrate control over dysfluencies by engaging in pseudostuttering. (13)

13. Model different dysfluent behaviors and ask the client to imitate them; ask him/her to read short passages and intentionally stutter on marked words, pause, and then say the target word fluently (I eat suh-suh-suh-salad. *Salad*).

7. Stutter more easily using the bounce technique. (13, 14, 15)

13. Model different dysfluent behaviors and ask the client to imitate them; ask him/her to read short passages and intentionally stutter on marked words, pause, and then say the target word fluently (I eat suh-suh-suh-salad. *Salad*).

14. Instruct the client in light articulatory placement of the lips and tongue to reduce the severity of tension in the production of plosives /p/, /b/, /t/, /k/, /g/ in the initial position

of words; practice articulation drills using light placement.

15. Using intentional stuttering and light articulatory contact, teach the client to bounce easily and slowly on stuttered syllables ("Buh-buh-buh-ball"); after the client masters the bounce, extend practice to the phrase and sentence levels; instruct the client to use the bounce in conversation when stuttering is anticipated.

8. Anticipate and circumvent the stuttering moment by readjusting muscular preparatory sets. (16, 17)

16. Instruct the client in self-monitoring skills to determine which physical conditions (e.g., muscle tension or autonomic signals) indicate the potential onset of a stuttering moment.

17. Using anticipatory cues, teach the client to slow his/her rate of speech before an expected stuttered word, to use an easy onset or bounce on the target word, and then extend the controlled dysfluency into the word that follows until the speech rate returns to normal.

9. Reestablish control of fluency after the stuttering moment using cancellations or pullouts. (18, 19)

18. Teach the client the *pullout* by instructing him/her to catch the stuttered word at its initiation, slow down the rate of the dysfluency, and, without pausing, bring the word to completion ("Wuh-wuh-wwwater").

19. Instruct the client that he/she should pause after a stuttered word and analyze the behaviors of the dysfluency, decide what alterations to make, then repeat the word with the appropriate

alterations (Dysfluency: "Wuh-wuh-wuh-water." Pause: relax, plan. Cancellation: "Wwwater").

10. Promote fluency by reducing the rate of speech. (20, 21)

20. Teach the client to reduce his/her rate of speech to a level at which stuttering does not occur by asking him/her to read passages at 60 words per minute (wpm); gradually increase the number of wpms, maintaining fluency at each level, until reaching 120 to 150 wpm.

21. Ask the client to read a passage backward to get the feel of slow verbal output; ask him/her to read the passage forward, keeping the feel of the reduced rate of speech.

11. Achieve fluency by using rhythmic speech. (22)

22. After setting a metronome at a slow rate, model speaking at a rate of one syllable per beat, asking the client to imitate while increasing the rate of the metronome incrementally; when an acceptable rate is reached without stuttering, fade the metronome by first initiating speech with it ticking, then turning it off, prompting the client to continue speaking at that rate; finally, before initiating speech, establish the rate with the metronome, turn it off, and ask the client to speak at that rate.

12. Achieve fluency systematically by gradually increasing the length and complexity of utterances. (23)

23. Ask the client to read a list of single words, stopping him/her if a word is stuttered; model correct production of the word, ask the client to say it fluently, and then continue; follow this procedure, gradually increasing the length of utterances while

13. Reduce cluttering by increasing intelligibility, speaking slowly, and adding emphasis to unstressed syllables 95% of the time. (24, 25, 26)

14. Maintain at least 95% fluency in a variety of speaking situations in everyday settings. (27, 28, 29)

maintaining 90% to 95% fluency.

24. After modeling slow speech with exaggerated articulation, ask the client to imitate while reading brief passages and while speaking spontaneously; agree on a signal system (e.g., a raised hand) to indicate that he/she should slow down and speak more distinctly when his/her rate and intelligibility become unacceptable.

25. Use modeling and behavior rehearsal to teach the client to make exaggerated pauses between phrases and sentences in reading and spontaneous speech; use a signal system to indicate when he/she is not pausing sufficiently.

26. Use modeling and behavior rehearsal to teach the client to speak with increased emphasis on syllables that are normally unstressed; use a signal system to indicate that he/she should add more stress to syllables when reading or speaking.

27. Encourage the client to develop self-monitoring skills by asking him/her to keep a log of speaking situations and chart the dysfluencies that occur; process the journal material to identify a coping technique that could be implemented in the future.

28. Teach the client's family and significant others to identify fluency breakdown and to promote fluent speech by

prompting, modeling, and reinforcing appropriate speech.

29. Accompany the client on excursions outside of the clinic to ensure that he/she has carried over fluent speech to everyday situations and consistently uses self-monitoring strategies.

__. _____   __. _____

_____   _____

__. _____   __. _____

_____   _____

__. _____   __. _____

_____   _____

DIAGNOSTIC SUGGESTIONS:

Axis I: 307.0   Stuttering
                 307.9   Communication Disorder NOS

                 _____   _____

                 _____   _____

HEARING IMPAIRMENT

BEHAVIORAL DEFINITIONS

1. Hearing loss in the range from 35 to 70 dB (has some residual hearing).
2. Sensorineural or mixed conductive and sensorineural loss.
3. Receptive and expressive language deficits.
4. Phonological impairment.
5. Prosodic features may include slow speaking rate, disturbed stress patterns, distorted resonance, and inadequate breath control.
6. Inattention to auditory signals.

—. _____

_____

—. _____

_____

—. _____

_____

LONG-TERM GOALS

1. Communicate needs and wants in daily routine situations.
2. Increase awareness and discrimination of different stimuli.
3. Use key vocabulary in daily communication.
4. Use conventional morphology and syntax during interactions with others.
5. Use appropriate social pragmatic communication in interactions with others.
6. Use age-appropriate phonological skills in conversations.
7. Use sign language to interact effectively with others in daily routines.

—. _____

   _____

—. _____

   _____

—. _____

   _____

SHORT-TERM OBJECTIVES

1. Participate willingly in a speech and language assessment. (1, 2, 3, 4)

THERAPEUTIC INTERVENTIONS

1. Administer standardized speech-language tests (e.g., Grammatical Analysis of Elicited Language by Moog, Kozak, and Geers; Rhode Island Test of Language Structure by Engen and Engen; or the Carolina Picture Vocabulary Test by Layton and Holmes) and criterion-referenced tests to determine the client's overall speech-language strengths and weaknesses; compare his/her speech-language development to dialectal, cultural, and developmental norms.

2. Before initiating the assessment of the client to determine if he/she should be tested in oral and/or sign language modalities, identify the appropriate comparison group for norm-referenced tests, modify the test as necessary without violating the norms, ensure that he/she understands the directions for the test, and minimize environmental distractions.

3. Administer a phonological test to determine the client's use of

phonology and an intelligibility test to determine how well others understand the client (e.g., Children's Speech Intelligibility Measure [CSIM] by Wilcox and Morris; Speech Intelligibility Evaluation by Monsen or the NTID Speech; and Voice Rating Scales by Subtelny, Orlando, and Whitehead).

4. Videotape a communication sample that represents the client's typical means of communication while engaged in his/her favorite routine activity that requires interaction; analyze the sample for his/her speech and language patterns (e.g., preintentional, intentional, gestural, signed, or verbal interactions with others).

2. Parents and teachers provide data regarding the client's history, medical status, communication skills, and hearing impairment consequences. (5, 6, 7)

5. Interview the client's parents, teacher, classroom aide, and other relevant academic professionals to determine his/her social and academic strengths and weaknesses.

6. Obtain observational data to document the client's communicative skills in the classroom, playground, cafeteria, vocational, community, home, and/or other critical social and academic situations.

7. Ask the parents to provide information on the client's developmental milestones, early communication characteristics, current medical status and history, previous professional intervention, communicative attempts in different settings,

and relevant social and family concerns.

3. Cooperate with an oral-motor examination. (8)

8. Evaluate the client's oral-motor skills by first observing the visible structure of his/her face, lips, teeth, tongue, and hard and soft palate; assess how he/she uses specific structures important for speech and language production (e.g., movement, strength, and closure of the lips; strength, protrusion, retraction and lateralization of the tongue; or movement of the soft palate when producing the /a/ phoneme).

4. Participate willingly in periodic audiological evaluations. (9)

9. Refer the client to an audiologist for routine evaluations.

5. Parents and teachers accept the recommendations given and collaboratively select a general communication mode and specific language targets. (10, 11, 12)

10. Conduct a meeting with parents and other professionals; first, to determine the client's eligibility for services; second, to develop collaborative intervention strategies; and, third, to determine the most appropriate general therapeutic approach, such as total, oral, or ASL communication programs for his/her individual needs.

11. Collaboratively select an intervention approach with the client's parents (e.g., oral, total, and/or manual signed approach) to help the client develop communication skills.

12. Select daily routines, specific vocabulary, word/sentence structures, and/or pragmatic situations as targets for intervention based on the client's hearing ability, chronological age, phonological

or motor skills; speech intelligibility, dialect, and social, vocational, and/or academic communicative needs; obtain the endorsement of parents and teachers for the intervention plan.

6. Use amplification and assistive devices to enhance auditory skills. (13, 14, 15)

13. Parents, audiologist, teachers, and the SLP collaboratively assist with identifying appropriate amplification and assistive listening devices for different situations and educate the client on the proper maintenance and care of these devices.

14. Check the status of the client's assistive listening device before the beginning of each treatment session.

15. Teach the client, with the assistance of the audiologist and/or the teacher consultant, to routinely check whether his/her listening device is working properly and how to remedy problems with the device, such as dead batteries or improper earmold seals.

7. Parents accept the client's level of speech and language skills relative to his/her hearing loss, development, physical status, and/or cognitive ability. (16, 17)

16. Explain to the client's parents, teachers, and other relevant professionals, the relationships between speech and language development and hearing loss, age, cognition, and physical status.

17. Provide helpful references and resources on hearing impairment and communication disorders for the client's parents and teachers (see the American Speech-Language-Hearing Association at

8. Parents and teachers advocate the client's inclusion in mainstream educational and recreational activities with age-appropriate peers. (18, 19)

9. Parents use communicative interactions that are contingent on the client's responses during daily routines. (20)

10. Indicate the presence or absence of sound with 90% accuracy. (21, 22, 23)

http://www.asha.org or the International Hearing Society at http://www.ihsinfo.org.

18. Help the parents and teachers advocate resources, such as instructional paraprofessional aides and curriculum adaptations, to enable the client to be included successfully in classrooms with age-appropriate, typically developing peers.

19. Assist with developing a social group that includes activities such as the client and age-appropriate peers meeting for recreational activities during lunch hours and after school.

20. Teach the client's parents to reduce the frequency of their directives and control of topics and to begin using an interactive language style that encourages the client to participate in conversations by using effective communicative strategies (e.g., *expansion:* saying a more mature version of the child's previous utterance, *turnabout:* acknowledging their child's previous utterance and then asking a question that extends the current topic, or *contingent query:* asking their child to repeat or clarify what he/she just said).

21. Ask the client to indicate when you have turned his/her hearing aid or other assistive listening device on or off.

22. Ask the client to signal when a sound starts and when it stops.

23. Train the client to respond to loud environmental sounds, such

11. Attend to sound appropriately 9 out of 10 times. (24, 25)

12. Discriminate between two different familiar environmental sounds with 80% accuracy. (26)

13. Discriminate between different spoken words with 80% accuracy. (27, 28, 29)

as banging on a hard surface or knocking on the door.

24. Using engaging toys that make sounds and movements, wait for the client to establish eye contact with you or the toy and then start the toy; when he/she turns his/her attention elsewhere, turn the toy off and then turn it back on when the client again establishes joint attention.

25. After the client attends to a toy that moves and makes sounds, hide the toy or put it behind his/her back and wait for him/her to turn toward the sound; if he/she does not respond, first, turn the volume up to get a response and then gradually reduce the volume to the lowest level the client can hear.

26. After choosing recorded environmental sounds that are familiar to the client, demonstrate two of the sounds and point to pictures that represent each sound then play the sounds and ask him/her to point to the correct picture after he/she hears the sound.

27. Teach the client to indicate which common phrase he/she hears by signing or gesturing what he/she hears (e.g., "bye-bye," "I'm hungry" or "more ____").

28. Teach the parents to help the client listen to common phrases during daily routines by presenting the phrases during everyday conversations (e.g., teach the parents to consistently

say, "Throw the ball" when playing with a ball. See the SKI-HI Program by Watkins and Clark for additional family-based interventions).

29. Choose words and phrases that the client needs in his/her classroom; provide pictures that represent spoken speech and train the client to listen carefully to identify pictures that match what he/she hears (e.g., "chair" and "share" or "bat" and "cat").

14. Expand frequency and range of signed communication. (30, 31, 32)

30. Teach the client, his/her parents, siblings, and significant others in his/her life to use manual communication signs, first, for needs and wants and then for important people and objects in his/her everyday routines; finally, continue to expand their use of vocabulary and syntax as needed.

31. Ask peers who sign proficiently to play and interact with the client on a regular basis.

32. Use manual signs within treatment sessions to improve the client's overall communication skills.

15. Demonstrate comprehension of oral and/or visual directions with 80% accuracy. (33, 34)

33. Teach the client vocabulary commonly used in oral and written directions (e.g., "top," "bottom," "before," or "first") by practicing these words with body motions and with paper and pencil tasks.

34. Play Simon Says by using directions with one, two, or three steps (e.g., "put your left hand on your stomach, your right hand on your head, and tap

16. Comprehend and speak key vocabulary needed for communication in the home, school, community, and/or vocational settings with 80% accuracy. (35, 36)

17. Engage in conversations about past and future familiar events. (37, 38)

your left foot); use visual cues first until the client achieves greater success.

35. Teach the parents strategies to expose the client to new vocabulary during daily activities in different settings (e.g., extending the client's utterance with additional semantic information, recasting his/her utterance into a different type of utterance, or parallel talk that provides the utterances for him/her during an activity).

36. Help the client make a reference notebook of the vocabulary words needed for his/her academic subjects or vocational settings; first, teach him/her to write the definitions of the vocabulary words in simple terms and then help him/her practice using those words in different oral and written contexts.

37. To develop the client's early narrative skills, instruct his/her parents to discuss past and future events in his/her life during daily interactions or by using pictures of him/her participating in different significant activities (e.g., birthday parties, vacations, or holidays).

38. To help the client learn to sequence and discuss daily activities, make a daily routine book that chronicles his/her activities throughout the day; teach him/her to describe what he/she did and what he/she will do in the future.

18. Improve use of correct syntax in conversations with 80% accuracy. (39, 40, 41)

39. For younger clients, teach parents to extend the client's utterances naturally in everyday conversations by adding slightly more complex syntax structures (e.g., saying, "Where is Mommy's hat?" when the client says "Where Mommy's hat?").

40. Write different parts of speech (e.g., noun and verb phrases, infinitive phrases, relative clauses, and prepositional phrases) on flashcards; teach the client to arrange different parts of speech to make various complex sentences.

41. For older clients, use written classroom homework to help him/her evaluate the syntax structures (e.g., transition markers between ideas) and elaborated noun and verb phrases, conjunctions, and different types of phrases and clauses.

19. Improve speech sound production with 80% intelligibility. (42)

42. Teach the client to use phonological skills that enable him/her to interact effectively in everyday situations (see the Phonological Disorders chapter in this *Planner* for specific interventions).

20. Ask for clarification when communication breaks down. (43, 44)

43. First, help the client to recognize when he/she did not hear or understand another speaker and then teach him/her appropriate language for requesting others to clarify the misunderstanding in conversations in different situations (e.g., saying, "What?, I don't understand," or "I'm sorry. I didn't hear you").

44. After purposefully leaving out critical information needed for completing an unfamiliar activity (e.g., building a structure, baking cookies, or doing an art project), first, prompt the client to state that he/she does not understand and then to ask clarification questions (e.g., "What do you want me to do?" "How does this fit?" or "Where does this go?").

21. Use appropriate social communication in school, work, and/or community settings. (45)

45. Use role play to teach the client conversational skills (e.g., introducing, maintaining or changing a topic, politeness markers, truthfulness, and relevance) the client needs to use in typical social situations.

__. _____

_____

__. _____

_____

__. _____

_____

__. _____

_____

__. _____

_____

__. _____

_____

DIAGNOSTIC SUGGESTIONS:

Axis I: 307.9   Communication Disorder NOS
            315.32   Mixed Receptive-Expressive Language
                     Disorder
            315.39   Phonological Disorder

            _____   _____

            _____   _____

Axis II: _____   _____

            _____   _____

INFANTS AT-RISK

BEHAVIORAL DEFINITIONS

1. Identified at risk from birth to 24-months for developmental disorders because of birth-related, endogenous, or exogenous factors (e.g., prematurity, potential congenital and inherited disorders, possible mental retardation, maternal substance abuse and/or abuse and neglect, or possible hearing impairment).
2. Consistent and significant delays in achieving developmental milestones.
3. Consistent and significant difficulty maintaining physiological and attentional states.
4. Consistent and significant difficulty with feeding, swallowing, and oral motor development.
5. Significant delay in development of vocalization.
6. Consistent and significant delay in development of age-appropriate communicative interactions with others.

—. _____
_____
_____
—. _____
_____
_____
—. _____
_____

LONG-TERM GOALS

1. Develop parental understanding of infant states that are optimal for communicative interactions.
2. Develop age-appropriate feeding patterns.
3. Develop age-appropriate vocalization patterns.

4. Develop age-appropriate comprehension skills.
5. Develop responsive turn-taking, imitation, and joint attention skills.
6. Understand and produce one- to two-word utterances, as developmentally appropriate.
7. Parents establish realistic expectations for their child's overall developmental ability and work collaboratively with their child's treatment professionals.

—. _____
_____
—. _____
_____
—. _____
_____

SHORT-TERM OBJECTIVES

1. Parents and other transdisciplinary professionals participate in administering standardized and criterion-referenced assessments and collecting ecological observational data on the client's development. (1, 2, 3, 4, 5)

THERAPEUTIC INTERVENTIONS

1. Administer standardized language tests (e.g., Bayley Scales of Infant Mental Development-Revised, Pre-Speech Assessment Scale, the Rossetti Infant-Toddler Language Scale, or the Vineland Adaptive Behavior Scales) to determine the client's overall developmental milestones and compare his/her behaviors to developmental norms.

2. Administer criterion-referenced tests to determine the client's specific feeding and pre-linguistic and linguistic skills defined as weaknesses by the standardized language tests for specifying long- and short-term objectives for intervention.

3. Videotape the client's interactions with significant others and analyze the tape for

his/her communication intentions, vocalizations, and first words, as developmentally appropriate.

4. Evaluate the client's oral-motor skills by first observing the visible structure of his/her face, lips, teeth, tongue, and hard and soft palate, and respiratory structures; assess how he/she uses specific structures important for later speech production (e.g., movement, strength, and closure of the lips during sucking).

5. Establish a measurable baseline of the client's feeding, prelinguistic, and/or behaviors before treatment begins.

2. Parents seek an audiological evaluation for the client. (6)

6. Refer the client to an audiologist for a hearing screening and, if indicated, a complete audiological evaluation.

3. Parents and other transdisciplinary professionals contribute information on the client's development and current status. (7)

7. Ask the parents and relevant professionals to provide information on the client's prenatal and postnatal developmental milestones, current medical status, and family concerns about coping with an at-risk infant.

4. Parents and other transdisciplinary professionals accept the recommendations given and collaboratively select specific communicative targets and general intervention strategies. (8, 9)

8. In partnership with the client's parents and other professionals (e.g., the nurse, physician, physical therapist, social worker, occupational therapist, and early childhood educator), determine his/her eligibility for services and develop collaborative intervention strategies.

9. Provide suggestions for procedures that positively assist the client's communication

5. Parents accept the client's communicative deficits relative to the developmental, cognitive, and physical status of their child; develop realistic expectations; and look for positive and supportive resources. (10, 11, 12)

6. Parents learn to recognize the preterm behavioral states and signs of stability that indicate the client's readiness for communication. (13)

7. Parents learn strategies for feeding the client and

development (e.g., monitoring his/her hearing and noise levels in the neonatal intensive care unit [NICU], weighing the risks of laryngeal damage from endotracheal tubes and benefits/risks of continued use of nasogastric and gavage tube feeding, reducing his/her sensory overstimulation from the bright lights, and emphasizing the importance of nonnutritive sucking and oral stimulation for his/her oral-motor development).

10. Explain to the client's parents and other professionals the relationships among communication development and age, cognition, and physical status.

11. Provide helpful references and resources on communication development for the client's parents (see the videotape and book, *Learning Language and Loving It* by Weitzman or the book *It Takes Two to Talk* by Manolson).

12. Introduce the client's parents to other parents of infants at-risk for support or for facilitating their participation in a local support group.

13. Teach the parents to become competent observers of the client's behavior by learning to chart his/her behaviors (e.g., respirations, color, alertness, and movements of extremities) in the NICU.

14. Teach the parents feeding interventions (see the

encouraging oral-motor development. (14)

8. Maintain a consistent level of arousal and eye contact during communicative interactions. (15)

9. Increase the frequency of imitating others' gestures, actions, and vocalizations. (16, 17, 18)

10. Increase the frequency of communicative intentions at the prelinguistic level by

Dysphagia—Children chapter in this *Planner* for specific feeding interventions).

15. Instruct the parents to gently arouse the client during the optimal physiological state, gain his/her attention, and move closer to the client to establish face-to-face eye contact while producing familiar phrases or sounds similar to his/her vocalizations.

16. After teaching the parents about common infant cues, help the parents to recognize the client's signals that indicate he/she is ready to interact (e.g., gazing at the parent or making cooing sounds); instruct the parent to imitate or match the client's vocal or physical behavior (e.g., cooing or coughing sounds or yawning and stretching movements) and then wait for the client to perform another or the same behavior that the parent may again imitate.

17. Instruct the parents to follow the client's lead during key play and social activities and then respond contingently to his/her communicative attempts to encourage increased communicative interactions.

18. Teach the parents to encourage the client to imitate actions during common play routines (e.g., playing Patty Cake, Peek-a-Boo, or So Big).

19. Arrange toys slightly out of reach so that the client must get the adult's attention, protest, or

producing more sophisticated babbling, vocalizations, and/or gestures. (19, 20, 21)

request the objects by using eye gaze, reaching movements, and/or vocalizations.

20. Change the interactive play routine in a surprising manner (e.g., first, giving the client blocks one at a time to put in a can and then quietly giving him/her a different small toy instead of a block to put in a can); model the appropriate communication intention for him/her (e.g., protesting, requesting, or responding).

21. After teaching the parents about the development of early phonology, instruct the parents to engage in vocal play with the client by first imitating his/her babbling behavior and then upping the ante to the use of the next developmental level of babbling with him/her (e.g., moving from consonant-vowel combinations to canonical babbling).

11. Increase frequency of communicative intentions of the one-word utterance. (22)

22. Focus on getting the client to use one- to two-word utterances (e.g., semantic utterances, such as agent, action, object, or possession) by selecting high-interest toys, such as a wind-up toy or bubbles; first, model utterances that reflect one-word semantic relationships (e.g., "go," "blow," or "bubbles"); second, ask him/her to imitate your model; and finally, wait expectantly for him/her to request continued action by saying the utterance (e.g., expect the child to say or approximate the word "blow" before blowing more bubbles).

12. Demonstrate an understanding of developmentally appropriate and relevant vocabulary up to at least 50 to 150 vocabulary words. (23)

13. Begin to use vocabulary in one- to two-word utterances, as developmentally appropriate. (24, 25)

14. Parents learn to use at least three different strategies for teaching the client to increase the length of his/her utterances, as developmentally appropriate. (26)

15. Demonstrate age-appropriate symbolic play by pretending to use common objects

23. Instruct the client to point to pictures in a simple picture book that represent target vocabulary words in response to questions (e.g., "Where's the doggy?").

24. After making a picture book of the client's everyday objects (e.g., his/her bed, chair, bathtub, toys, books, eating utensils, or other items he/she uses frequently), first, ask the client to imitate words that he/she may frequently use in his/her environment (e.g., "say _____") and then ask the client to answer, "What's this?" questions that elicit the labels of the objects.

25. Teach the client's parents to frequently model common vocabulary items in one to two-word phrases during everyday routines such as eating dinner (e.g., "want beans?"), taking a bath (e.g., "wash face"), or changing clothes (e.g., "your shirt," "your pants").

26. Teach the parents to use communicative strategies with the client (e.g., *expansion:* saying a more mature version of the child's previous utterance, *turnabout:* acknowledging their child's previous utterance and then asking a question that extends the current topic, or *contingent query:* asking the child to repeat or clarify what he/she just said).

27. During play activities, teach the client to imitate actions associated with common

correctly with 80% accuracy. (27)

household objects (e.g., pretending to use a telephone, comb hair, sweep the floor, use a toothbrush, or eat from a spoon).

16. Demonstrate an understanding of the meaning of early basic concept vocabulary as developmentally appropriate with 80% accuracy. (28)

28. Provide practice for the client on early spatial words (e.g., on, down, in, out of) while playing with simple manipulative toys.

__. _____

__. _____

__. _____

__. _____

__. _____

__. _____

DIAGNOSTIC SUGGESTIONS:

Axis I: 307.59   Feeding Disorder of Infancy or Childhood
307.9   Communication Disorder NOS

_____ _____

_____ _____

LANGUAGE DISORDERS—
ADOLESCENTS

BEHAVIORAL DEFINITIONS

1. Receptive and/or expressive vocabulary is substantially below expected developmental norms for typically developing 13- to 18-year-old adolescents.
2. Consistent and significant difficulty with comprehending and/or producing oral and written language.
3. Consistent and significant deficits with understanding and producing complex sentences.
4. Consistent and significant difficulty with the meaning and organization of language.
5. Consistent and significant difficulty with the use of pragmatic functions of language.
6. Language deficits interfere significantly with effective communication at home, school, and in the community.

—. _____
   _____
—. _____
   _____
—. _____
   _____

LONG-TERM GOALS

1. Develop an understanding of and produce academic and vocational vocabulary in diverse communicative contexts appropriate for age, dialect, and cultural expectations.

2. Organize vocabulary into semantic categories for efficient retrieval and subsequent use.
3. Understand and produce complex sentences appropriate for age, dialect, and cultural expectations in conversations.
4. Use pragmatic skills appropriate for age, dialect, and cultural expectations in various communicative contexts.
5. Use cognitive strategies for retaining and using the language necessary for academic and vocational success.
6. Parents and client establish realistic expectations for the client's language skills.

—. _____
   _____
   _____
—. _____
   _____
   _____
—. _____
   _____

SHORT-TERM OBJECTIVES

1. Participate willingly in a language assessment. (1, 2, 3, 4, 5)

THERAPEUTIC INTERVENTIONS

1. Administer standardized language tests to determine the client's overall receptive and expressive language strengths and weaknesses and to compare his/her language development to dialectal, cultural, and developmental norms.

2. Administer criterion-referenced tests to determine the client's specific language skills in the linguistic areas defined as weaknesses by the standardized language tests.

3. Videotape or audiotape a language sample and ask the client to write a paragraph or essay that represents the client's typical oral and written production; analyze these

samples for the client's use of language skills.

4. Interview the client's teachers, the client, and other relevant professionals to determine social, academic, and vocational strengths and weaknesses of the client.

5. Document the client's communicative skills in classrooms, work-study contexts, or other critical academic and social situations.

2. Cooperate with an oral-motor examination. (6)

6. Evaluate the client's oral-motor skills by first observing the visible structure of his/her face, lips, teeth, tongue, hard and soft palate and then assess how he/she uses specific structures important for speech and language production (e.g., movement, strength, and closure of the lips; strength, protrusion, retraction, and lateralization of the tongue; or movement of the soft palate when producing the /a/ phoneme).

3. Participate willingly in an audiological evaluation. (7, 8)

7. Conduct a pure-tone audiological screening at 500 Hz, 1000 Hz, 2000 Hz, and 4000 Hz at 20 dB for the client.

8. Refer the client to an audiologist for a complete evaluation if results of the audiological screening indicate a need for further assessment.

4. Parents participate in the evaluation process and contribute to the interpretation of evaluation information. (9, 10, 11)

9. Ask the parents to provide information on the client's current medical status and history; previous professional intervention; communication ability in different academic,

vocational, and social settings; and relevant social and family concerns.

10. Parents seek a medical evaluation for the client from a physician to identify any organic bases for the language disorder.

11. Parents seek a cognitive evaluation for the client from an educational psychologist to identify cognitive deficits.

5. Parents and the client accept the recommendations given and collaboratively select language targets and a general intervention strategy. (12, 13, 14)

12. Conduct a meeting with the parents, client, and other relevant professionals first, to determine the client's eligibility for services and, second, to develop collaborative intervention strategies.

13. Determine the most appropriate general therapeutic approach (e.g., individual or group, collaborative, consultative, course for credit, or pull-out) for the client's individual needs.

14. Select specific vocabulary words, word/sentence structures, cognitive strategies and/or pragmatic situations as targets for intervention based on the client's age, dialect, social, academic, and vocational communicative needs.

6. Parents and teachers accept the client's language deficits relative to the developmental, cognitive and physical status of the client, develop realistic expectations, and look for positive and supportive resources. (15, 16)

15. Explain to the client, his/her parents, teachers, and other relevant professionals, the relationships among language development and age, speech development, cognition, and physical status.

16. Provide helpful references and resources on language development and disorders for

7. Identify consequences that may be used to reinforce progress. (17)

8. Verbalize an understanding of how specific therapeutic interventions contribute to better language skills and how these skills ultimately lead to effective communication. (18, 19)

9. Identify the classroom teachers' main and supporting ideas and the teachers' verbal and non-verbal cues that signal important information. (20)

10. Follow three-step oral and/or written directions correctly with 100% accuracy. (21)

the client, his/her parents and teachers (see Internet resources from the American Speech-Language-Hearing Association http://www.asha.org).

17. Explore consequences that may be used to reinforce the client's successful communicative attempts with him/her (e.g., verbal praise, an academic grade, or a language progress contract).

18. Before beginning an activity, clearly state the therapeutic goal of the activity for the client (e.g., "Now we will learn to use two new strategies to help you remember what your science teacher wants you to learn"); at the end of the activity, ask him/her to tell you the specific goal for that activity and how it relates to overall communicative success.

19. After the client uses language targets during intervention, ask him/her to make judgments about the quality of his/her language performance with 100% accuracy.

20. Teach the client how to identify main and supporting ideas by using newspaper articles, academic texts, and/or brief video/audio recorded lectures; instruct him/her to use different strategies for keeping notes efficiently.

21. Teach the client to use strategies for remembering three-step directions the first time he/she hears them (e.g., repeating the

directions quietly, writing a brief note or graphic symbol, and/or making nonverbal motions to represent the main idea of each step) as he/she hears or reads the directions.

11. Define and appropriately use vocabulary in context as needed for academic, social and, if appropriate, vocational success. (22, 23, 24)

22. Ask the client to keep a reference notebook of the vocabulary words needed for his/her academic subjects or vocational settings; first, teach him/her to write the definitions of the vocabulary words in simple terms and then to write two or three sentences that use each word appropriately.

23. Using the client's academic texts, identify difficult vocabulary words with him/her and then teach him/her how to define and remember these words by using different strategies (e.g., writing the words and definitions on separate index cards and then matching the words to their corresponding definitions).

24. Teach the client how to look for root words and affixes (e.g., divine and divinity) in his/her academic texts and discuss meaning differences that depend on a particular affix; instruct him/her to maintain a list of root words and their possible meanings.

12. Verbally sort, compare, and contrast curriculum-based vocabulary words to an accuracy of 90%. (25, 26)

25. Teach the client to use visual drawings (e.g., semantic word webs, Venn diagrams, and other logical visual organizations) for grouping, comparing, and contrasting curriculum-based

words in meaningful semantic categories.

26. Have the client sort curriculum-based vocabulary words into groups based on similar characteristics; ask him/her to state the common features or superordinate category for each group.

13. Say or write sentences that include the correct use of idioms with 80% accuracy as appropriate for developmental age. (27, 28)

27. Instruct the client to illustrate the figurative meanings of idioms, metaphors, or similes (e.g., "letting the cat out of the bag," "as the crow flies," "bull-headed," or "as free as a bird"); ask him/her to say or write sentences that include the correct use of the idioms.

28. Using comic strips, cartoons, puns, and/or jokes, help the client understand the figurative meaning of humorous vocabulary that particularly includes multiple meanings then teach him/her to share his/her favorite type of humor in a socially acceptable manner.

14. Rephrase and accurately state the meanings of complex sentences in own words. (29)

29. Teach the client to understand the components of oral and/or written complex sentences, such as relative and infinitive clauses, adverbial and prepositional phrases, elaborated noun phrases, gerunds, and passive sentences.

15. Produce verbal and/or written forms of complex sentences, as appropriate for developmental age. (30, 31)

30. Write different parts of speech (e.g., noun and verb phrases, infinitive phrases, relative clauses, and prepositional phrases) on flashcards; and teach the client to arrange the different parts in order to make various complex sentences.

31. Assist the client in reviewing his/her written narratives or essays and evaluate the syntax structures (e.g., transition markers between ideas, elaborated noun and verb phrases, conjunctions, and different types of phrases and clauses).

16. Initiate and respond to others with various speech acts such as greetings, introductions, and requests. (32)

32. Ask the client to role-play situations that use conversational skills (e.g., introducing, maintaining, or changing a topic; politeness markers; truthfulness; and relevance) he/she needs to use in typical adolescent social situations.

17. Request others to clarify misunderstandings in conversations. (33)

33. After purposefully leaving out critical information needed for completing an unfamiliar activity (e.g., building a structure, performing a vocational skill, or completing a hobby or craft); first, prompt the client to state that he/she does not understand and then prompt the client to ask clarification questions such as, "What do you want me to do?" "How does this fit?" or "Where does this go?"

18. Self-repair misunderstandings in conversations by rephrasing or restating. (34)

34. Have the client give oral directions to a peer (e.g., how to play games or how to drive a car or other age-appropriate tasks) with limited use of nonverbal cues then teach the client how to rephrase oral directions that are confusing.

19. Answer 90% of questions correctly to demonstrate comprehension of curriculum-based narrative and expository texts. (35, 36)

35. Teach the client strategies (e.g., anticipating content by scanning headings and subheadings, making a list of questions about the readings, or paraphrasing the

important content) for compre-hending information in written texts (see *Language Disorders from Infancy through Adolescence* by Paul).

36. Using age-appropriate novels, teach the client how to summarize, predict, and evaluate the characters and events of the story; test his/her comprehension by asking relevant questions about the content presented.

20. Tell or write narratives and expository essays using high-level syntax constructions. (37, 38)

37. After reading a story to the client, ask him/her to retell events of a story by incrementally adding more details and narrative structures; use visual strategies (e.g., making an outline or a series of graphic symbols and pictures) to help the client organize the story and tape-record his/her production so that he/she can critically evaluate his/her performance.

38. Teach the client to tell past personal narratives in a culturally and socially appropriate manner (e.g., for a client from mainstream American culture; instruct the client to get and maintain the listener's attention; set the scene; tell the events in a logical, sequential order; use evaluative and cohesive devices; and describe consequences and reactions).

21. Use cohesive markers correctly in oral and written narrative and expository texts. (39)

39. Instruct the client to keep a list of useful connectives and cohesive words (e.g., pronouns and different types of con-

junctions, such as "but," "although," or "however") to use when writing curriculum-based assignments, teach the client to refer to the list and include appropriate connectives and cohesive devices in his/her assignment.

—. _____   —. _____
     _____   _____
—. _____   —. _____
     _____   _____
—. _____   —. _____
     _____   _____

DIAGNOSTIC SUGGESTIONS:

Axis I: 315.31   Expressive Language Disorder
                   315.32   Mixed Receptive-Expressive Language
                               Disorder

                   _____   _____

                   _____   _____

LANGUAGE DISORDERS—CHILDREN

BEHAVIORAL DEFINITIONS

1. Receptive and/or expressive vocabulary is substantially below expected developmental norms for typically developing 5- to 12-year-old children.
2. Consistent and significant difficulty with understanding and producing basic and complex syntax structures.
3. Consistent and significant deficits with understanding and/or producing morphological features.
4. Consistent and significant difficulty with the meaning and organization of language.
5. Consistent and significant difficulty with the use of pragmatic functions of language.
6. Language deficits interfere significantly with effective communication at home, school, and in the community.

—. _____

_____

—. _____

_____

—. _____

_____

LONG-TERM GOALS

1. Develop an understanding of and produce vocabulary in diverse communicative contexts appropriate for age, dialect, and cultural expectations.

2. Organize vocabulary into semantic categories for efficient retrieval and subsequent use.
3. Develop an understanding of and produce basic and complex sentences appropriate for age, dialect, and cultural expectations in conversations.
4. Develop an understanding of and produce morphological structures appropriate for age, dialect, and cultural expectations in conversations.
5. Use pragmatic skills appropriate for age, dialect, and cultural expectations in various communicative contexts.
6. Parents establish realistic expectations for their child's language skills.

—. _____
_____

—. _____
_____

—. _____
_____

SHORT-TERM OBJECTIVES

1. Participate willingly in a language assessment.
(1, 2, 3, 4, 5)

THERAPEUTIC INTERVENTIONS

1. Administer standardized language tests to determine the client's overall receptive and expressive language strengths and weaknesses and to compare his/her language development to dialectal, cultural, and developmental norms.

2. Administer criterion-referenced tests to determine the client's specific language skills in the linguistic areas defined as weaknesses by the standardized language tests.

3. Videotape or audiotape a language sample that represents the client's typical conversational production while discussing favorite topics and analyze

the sample for his/her use of language.

4. Interview the client's teacher, the client, if age-appropriate, and other relevant academic professionals to determine the client's social and academic strengths and weaknesses.

5. Document the client's communicative skills in the classroom, playground, cafeteria or other critical social and academic situations.

2. Cooperate with an oral-motor examination. (6)

6. Evaluate the client's oral-motor skills by first observing the visible structure of his/her face, lips, teeth, tongue, hard and soft palate, and then assess how he/she uses specific structures important for speech and language production (e.g., movement, strength, and closure of the lips; strength, protrusion, retraction, and lateralization of the tongue; or movement of the soft palate when producing the /a/ phoneme).

3. Participate willingly in an audiological evaluation. (7, 8)

7. Conduct a pure-tone audiological screening at 500 Hz, 1000 Hz, 2000 Hz, and 4000 Hz at 20 dB for the client.

8. Refer the client to an audiologist for a complete evaluation if results of the audiological screening indicate a need for further assessment.

4. Parents participate in the evaluation process and contribute to the interpretation of evaluation information. (9, 10, 11)

9. Ask the parents to provide information on the client's developmental milestones, current medical status and history, previous professional intervention, communicative

attempts in different settings, and relevant social and family concerns.

10. Parents seek a medical evaluation for the client from a pediatrician or an otolaryngologist (ear/nose/throat physician) to identify any organic bases for the language disorder.

11. Parents seek a cognitive evaluation for the client from an educational psychologist to identify cognitive development delays.

5. Parents accept the recommendations given, and collaboratively select language targets and a general intervention strategy. (12, 13, 14)

12. Conduct a meeting with parents and other relevant professionals, first, to determine the client's eligibility for services and, second, to develop collaborative intervention strategies.

13. Determine the most appropriate general therapeutic approach (e.g., collaborative, consultative, or pull-out therapy) for the client's individual needs.

14. Select specific vocabulary, word/sentence structures, and/or pragmatic situations as targets for intervention based on the client's age, phonological skills, speech intelligibility, dialect, and social and academic communicative needs.

6. Parents and teachers accept the client's language deficits relative to his/her developmental, cognitive, and physical status, develop realistic expectations, and look for positive and supportive resources. (15, 16)

15. Explain to the client's parents, teachers, and other relevant professionals, the relationships among language development and age, speech development, cognition, and physical status.

16. Provide helpful references and resources on language development and disorders for the client's parents and teachers

7. Parents, teachers and, if appropriate, the client assist with identifying consequences that may be used to reinforce progress. (17)

8. Verbalize an understanding of how specific therapeutic interventions contribute to better language skills, and how these skills ultimately lead to effective communication.(18, 19)

9. Follow three-step oral and/or written directions correctly with 100% accuracy. (20, 21)

(see Internet resources from the American Speech-Language-Hearing Association at http://www.asha.org).

17. Explore with the client's parents, teachers, and the client consequences that may be used to reinforce the client's successful communicative attempts, such as extrinsic reinforcers (e.g., verbal praise or other redeemable tokens) and intrinsic reinforcers (e.g., receiving an immediate response to a clearly verbalized request).

18. Before beginning an activity, clearly state the therapeutic goal of the activity for the client (e.g., "We are learning about prepositional phrases to help you make better sentences"); at the end of the activity, ask the client to tell you the specific goal for that activity and how it relates to communicative success.

19. After the client uses language targets during intervention, ask him/her to make judgments about the quality of his/her language performance.

20. Teach the client common spatial and temporal vocabulary (e.g., "next to," "before," or "after") in two- and three-step directions and then provide visual, motor, or auditory strategies to help him/her remember the sequence of directions, first, using familiar tasks such as common classroom or home routines and then using less familiar, novel tasks (e.g., making a paper airplane or making cookies).

10. Demonstrate an understanding of relationships between root words and their suffixes and prefixes. (22, 23)

11. Use regular and irregular past tense verb forms appropriately in sentences with 80% accuracy. (24)

12. Produce regular and irregular plural forms appropriately in sentences with 80% accuracy. (25)

13. Use age-appropriate vocabulary in academic and social situations. (26)

21. Instruct the client to follow your directions that include multiple spatial and semantic terms (e.g., "Place the small yellow square in the middle of the large purple circle") while playing a barrier game consisting of matching sets of objects with different colors, sizes, and shapes.

22. Use sentence completion tasks to teach the client to contrast root words with age-appropriate contrasting prefixes or suffixes (e.g., " friendly" and "unfriendly" or "decline" and "incline") with 80% accuracy.

23. Instruct the client to make new words by matching various written forms of prefixes or suffixes (e.g., "un-," "-ness," "-ful," "-er," or "ly") with written forms of root words (e.g., " happy," "joy," or "safe") define and use those words with and without prefixes or suffixes in contrasting sentences.

24. Pantomime action words (e.g., "go," "ride," or "drive") and have the client state the irregular past tense forms of the action word he/she saw (e.g., "You just drove a car").

25. Instruct the client to match pictorial or written forms of singular and irregular plural nouns (e.g., " man" and "men" or " goose" and "geese") and then produce them in contrasting sentences.

26. Using the client's academic texts or age-appropriate narrative books, first identify important

vocabulary words and then discuss the meanings of those words in depth and, finally, teach him/her to use the same vocabulary words in oral and/or written contexts.

14. Verbally sort, compare, and contrast curriculum-based vocabulary words to an accuracy of 90%. (27, 28)

27. Teach the client to use visual drawings (e.g., semantic word webs, Venn diagrams, and other logical visual organizations) for grouping, comparing, or contrasting curriculum-based words in meaningful semantic categories.

28. Have the client sort curriculum-based objects or pictures into groups based on similar characteristics; ask him/her to state the common features or superordinate category for each group.

15. Choose the correct pictures that accurately represent particular oral and/or written forms of complex sentences with 80% accuracy. (29)

29. Teach the client an understanding of oral and/or written complex sentences, such as relative and infinitive clauses, adverbial and prepositional phrases, elaborated noun phrases, gerunds, and passive sentences.

16. Produce verbal and/or written forms of complex sentences, as appropriate for developmental age. (30, 31)

30. Ask the client to repeat and complete the phrases, "I went to a restaurant and I saw ____," "I went to the zoo and I saw ____," "I went to the beach and I saw ____," or "I went to the farm and I saw ____" and take turns adding subsequent additional phrase completions with elaborated noun phrases (e.g., "I went to the zoo and I saw funny, mischievous monkeys who were climbing and ferocious, wild lions who

were pacing") to encourage complex sentences.

31. Write different parts of speech (e.g., noun and verb phrases, infinitive phrases, relative clauses, and prepositional phrases) on flashcards; teach the client to arrange different parts of speech to make various complex sentences.

17. Initiate and respond to others with various speech acts such as greetings, introductions and requests. (32)

32. Model communicative routines (e.g., how to make introductions, greetings, or getting someone's attention) that are typical situations for the client; ask him/her to role-play the communicative situations appropriately.

18. Request others to clarify misunderstandings in conversations. (33)

33. After purposefully leaving out critical information needed for completing an unfamiliar activity (e.g., building a structure, baking cookies, or doing an art project), prompt the client to state that he/she does not understand and then to ask clarification questions (e.g., "What do you want me to do?" "How does this fit?" or "Where does this go?").

19. Self-repair misunderstandings in conversations by rephrasing or restating. (34)

34. Have the client give oral directions while playing a barrier game with a peer; teach him/her how to rephrase the oral directions that are confusing.

20. Answer 90% of questions correctly to demonstrate comprehension of curriculum-based narrative and expository texts. (35, 36)

35. Ask the client comprehension questions after telling or reading an age-appropriate, curriculum-based story (e.g., "What happened to the____?" "Why do you think he did that?" "Where he go after____?") "How do you

think he felt when that happened?").

36. Using age-appropriate narrative books, teach the client how to summarize, predict, and evaluate the characters and events of the story; test his/her comprehension by asking relevant questions about the content presented.

21. Tell increasingly more complex narratives using appropriate story structures for developmental age. (37, 38)

37. After reading a story to the client repeatedly, ask him/her to retell events of a story by incrementally adding more details and narrative structures, as culturally appropriate.

38. Reenact real-life scripts or events (e.g., having a birthday party or going to a restaurant); teach the client to write or verbalize the events with increasingly more sophisticated use of cohesive pronouns and transitions to connect the events.

__. _____   __. _____
    _____   _____
__. _____   __. _____
    _____   _____
__. _____   __. _____
    _____   _____

DIAGNOSTIC SUGGESTIONS:

Axis I: 315.31   Expressive Language Disorder
               315.32   Mixed Receptive-Expressive Language
                         Disorder

               _____   _____
               _____   _____

LANGUAGE DISORDERS— PRESCHOOLERS

BEHAVIORAL DEFINITIONS

1. Expressive vocabulary is substantially below expected developmental norms for typically developing 2- to 5-year-old children.
2. Consistent and significant difficulty with understanding basic syntax structures in conversations.
3. Consistent and significant difficulty producing basic syntax structures in conversations.
4. Significant deficit in the understanding of morphological features.
5. Significant deficit in the production of morphological features.
6. Consistent and significant difficulty with the use of pragmatic functions of language.
7. Language deficits interfere significantly with effective communication at home, preschool, and in the community.

—. _____
   _____
—. _____
   _____
—. _____
   _____

LONG-TERM GOALS

1. Develop an understanding of and produce vocabulary in diverse communicative contexts appropriate for age, dialect, and cultural expectations.

2. Develop an understanding of and produce basic syntax structures appropriate for age, dialect, and cultural expectations in conversations.
3. Develop an understanding of and produce morphological structures appropriate for age, dialect, and cultural expectations in conversations.
4. Use pragmatic skills appropriate for age, dialect, and cultural expectations in various communicative contexts.
5. Parents establish realistic expectations for their child's language skills.

—. _____
   _____

—. _____
   _____

—. _____
   _____

SHORT-TERM OBJECTIVES

THERAPEUTIC INTERVENTIONS

1. Participate willingly in a language assessment. (1, 2, 3, 4)

1. Administer standardized language tests to determine the client's overall receptive and expressive language strengths and weaknesses, and to compare his/her language development to dialect, cultural, and developmental norms.

2. Administer criterion-referenced tests to determine the client's specific language skills in the linguistic areas defined as weaknesses by the standardized language tests to determine specific long- and short-term objectives for intervention.

3. Videotape or audiotape a language sample that represents the client's typical conversational production while playing with interactive toys, and analyze the tape for his/her language skills.

2. Cooperate with an oral-motor examination. (5)

3. Participate willingly in an audiological evaluation. (6, 7)

4. Parents participate in the evaluation process and contribute to the interpretation of evaluation information. (8, 9, 10)

4. Establish a measurable baseline of the client's language skills before treatment begins.

5. Evaluate the client's oral-motor skills by first observing the visible structure of his/her face, lips, teeth, tongue, hard and soft palate and then assess how he/she uses specific structures important for speech and language production (e.g., movement, strength, and closure of the lips; strength, protrusion, retraction, and lateralization of the tongue; or movement of the soft palate when producing the /a/ phoneme).

6. Conduct a pure-tone audiological screening at 500 Hz, 1000 Hz, 2000 Hz, and 4000 Hz at 20 dB for the client.

7. Refer the client to an audiologist for a complete evaluation if results of the audiological screening indicate a need for further assessment.

8. Ask the parents to provide information on the client's developmental milestones, current medical status and history, previous professional intervention, communicative attempts in different settings, and relevant social and family concerns.

9. Parents seek a medical evaluation for the client from a pediatrician or an otolaryngologist (ear/nose/throat physician) to identify any organic bases for the language disorder.

5. Parents accept the recommendations given and collaboratively select language targets and a general intervention strategy. (11, 12, 13)

10. Parents seek a cognitive evaluation for the client from an educational psychologist to identify cognitive development delays.

11. Conduct a meeting with the parents, first, to determine the client's eligibility for services and, second, to develop collaborative intervention strategies.

12. Determine the most appropriate general therapeutic approach (i.e., clinician-directed, client-directed, parent-directed, or hybrid) for the client's individual needs.

13. Select specific vocabulary, word/sentence structures, and/or pragmatic situations as targets for intervention based on the client's age, phonological skills, speech intelligibility, dialect, and/or social and educational communicative needs.

6. Parents accept the client's language deficits relative to his/her developmental, cognitive and physical status, develop realistic expectations, and look for positive and supportive resources. (14, 15, 16)

14. Explain to the client's parents the relationships among language development and age, speech development, cognition, and physical status.

15. Provide helpful references and resources on language development and disorders for the client's parents (see Internet resources from the American Speech-Language-Hearing Association at http://www.asha.org).

16. Introduce the client's parents to other parents of children with language disorders for informal support or for facilitating their

participation in a local support group; refer his/her parents to a support group.

7. Parents assist with identifying consequences that may be used to reinforce progress. (17)

17. Explore with client's parents what consequences may be used to reinforce the client's successful communicative attempts (e.g., extrinsic reinforcers, such as food and redeemable tokens, or verbal praise and intrinsic reinforcers, such as receiving an immediate response to a clearly verbalized request).

8. Produce utterances that reflect two-word semantic relationships with 80% accuracy. (18)

18. Focus on getting the client to use two-word utterances (e.g., such as agent-action, action-object, agent object, or possession) by selecting a high-interest toy (e.g., a Fisher-Price fishing game or bubble-blowing liquid); first, model utterances that reflect two-word or semantic relationships (e.g., "catch fish," "more fish," or "big bubbles"); next, ask the child to imitate your model; and, finally, wait expectantly for the child to request continued action by saying the two-word utterance (e.g., expect the child to say, "more bubbles" before blowing more bubbles).

9. Demonstrate an understanding of and produce age-appropriate and relevant vocabulary with 80% accuracy. (19, 20)

19. Instruct the client to point to and say the names of pictures in a simple picture book or on lotto boards that represent target vocabulary words.

20. After making a picture book of the client's everyday objects (e.g., his/her bed, chair, bathtub, toys, books, eating utensils, or other items he/she uses

frequently) ask him/her questions to elicit verb responses (e.g., "What is your bed for?" "I sleep in it").

10. Demonstrate an understanding of meaning and accurately produce spatial, deictic, and temporal words. (21)

21. Provide practice on basic concept vocabulary focusing on spatial words (e.g., on, down, under, above), deictic words (e.g., this, that), and temporal words (e.g., after, before) by asking the client to imitate such phrases as "in the house," "out of the house," "on the swing," or "around the chair" while playing with a toy house with realistic furniture and people or other similar manipulative toys.

11. Demonstrate understanding of and verbally identify basic word classes, such as colors and other physical attributes of objects. (22)

22. Teach the client to produce descriptive vocabulary words (e.g., "these are red," ". . . round," or ". . . smooth") while grouping various objects of different colors, shapes, and textures.

12. Understand the meaning of and produce bound morphemes, such as -ing, -s, or -ed, with 80% accuracy. (23, 24, 25)

23. Instruct the client to choose pictures that represent the words he/she hears when shown pictures of minimal pair words (e.g., "walk" or "walks," "cat" or "cats") that highlight particular bound morphemes.

24. Ask the client to raise his/her hand, point to a smiley or sad face, or drop blocks in a bowl to indicate correct or incorrect usage of bound morphemes.

25. Use sentence completion tasks to teach the client to correctly produce words with bound morphemes while playing with objects or looking at pictures, which appropriately represent

13. Increase average utterance length as appropriate for developmental age. (26)

14. Display accurate understanding and usage of pronouns as appropriate for developmental age. (27)

15. Produce subjective and objective pronouns in sentences as appropriate for developmental age with 80% accuracy. (28)

16. Answer questions correctly to demonstrate comprehension of past, present, and future tenses of familiar verbs as appropriate for developmental age. (29)

17. Produce verb tenses in utterances as appropriate for developmental age. (30, 31)

bound morphemes, with 80% accuracy.

26. Model longer utterances, first, by repeating and increasing the length of the client's utterances by two to three additional appropriate words immediately after he/she says a short utterance and then subsequently ask him/her to repeat the longer utterance while engaged in creative activities (e.g., playing with favorite toys, making cookies, or reading books).

27. Instruct the client to point to the correct picture after listening to sentences that contrast the correct pronouns in the objective and subjective case (e.g., "He chased after her" and "She chased after him").

28. Teach the client to produce pronouns correctly eight out of ten times when referring to relatives or friends (e.g., "She is my sister" and "He is my neighbor") while looking at actual photographs.

29. Ask the client comprehension questions (e.g., "Did you just *jump?*") about his/her actions during familiar routines and include deliberate false assertions (e.g., ask, "Did you just *crawl?*" when he/she is jumping).

30. Ask the client to describe his/her own actions during familiar routines (e.g., eating snacks, playing with blocks, cars, other toys, or engaging in other typical activities).

18. Answer questions correctly to demonstrate understanding of negative, question, or complex sentence constructions. (32)

19. Produce questions, prepositional phrases or conjoined phrases as appropriate for developmental age. (33, 34, 35)

31. Using pictures or actual demonstrations of actions, ask the client to perform the action and then ask what he/she is doing presently, did previously, or what he/she will do next to elicit past, present, and future verb tenses.

32. Ask the client to choose the correct picture that accurately represents a particular prepositional phrase, negative statement, or complex utterance.

33. Ask the client to watch carefully and then produce various prepositional phrases that describe your actions (e.g., putting a doll in the bed, driving a car around the track, or throwing a ball through a basketball hoop).

34. Ask the client to repeat and complete the phrases (e.g., "I went to a restaurant and I saw ____," "I went to the zoo and I saw ____," "I went to the beach and I saw ____," or "I went to the farm and I saw ____") and take turns adding subsequent additional phrase completions (e.g., " I went to the zoo and I saw monkeys and lions and tigers") to encourage more complex sentences with conjoined phrases.

35. Teach the client to ask questions of others about their feelings or actions by using prompts (e.g., "Ask Mary how she feels" or "Why don't you ask Tom what he is doing?").

20. Initiate and respond to others with styles of speaking appropriate for different situations and/or conversational partners. (36)

21. Maintain topics for three to five turns in conversations with peers and adults. (37)

22. Use requests, comments, boasts, disagreements, or protests appropriately in conversations with peers and adults. (38)

23. Request others to clarify misunderstandings in conversations. (39, 40)

36. Using a toy house and dolls representing different ages, demonstrate appropriate and inappropriate ways to make or respond to requests when playacting different roles; ask the client to repeat appropriate requests or responses.

37. Choose a topic of high interest to the client and encourage him/her to continue the conversation for three to five turns, as appropriate for age, providing negative and positive prompts to teach him/her to stay on the same topic.

38. Using puppets or dolls, role-play familiar communicative routines that are typical situations for the client and demonstrate how to make requests, comments, boasts, disagreements, or protests appropriately and then switch roles and ask the child to role-play different speech acts appropriately.

39. After mumbling or talking too softly when completing everyday activities or tasks that require specific directions, encourage the client to ask for clarification by using a prompt (e.g., "Ask me what I said") to teach him/her age-appropriate, specific phrases for requesting clarification from others (e.g., "What did you say?").

40. Make intentional and obvious errors when completing tasks on play activities (e.g., putting the parts of Mr. Potato Head together) and then teach the child to produce age-appropriate

24. Tell age-appropriate
narratives. (41, 42, 43)

questions for clarifying content errors.

41. Reenact real-life scripts or events (e.g., having a birthday party or going to a restaurant) and then ask the client to correctly verbalize what he/she did in two to three sequential utterances.

42. Using pictures or photographs that illustrate two to three sequences of familiar events ask the client to put them in the proper order and tell the story.

43. Using age-appropriate narrative picture books, ask the client to summarize, predict, or evaluate the characters and events of the story.

__. _____   __. _____
    _____   _____
__. _____   __. _____
    _____   _____
__. _____   __. _____
    _____   _____

DIAGNOSTIC SUGGESTIONS:

Axis I: 315.31   Expressive Language Disorder
                 315.32   Mixed Receptive-Expressive Language
                           Disorder

                 _____   _____
                 _____   _____

MENTAL IMPAIRMENT

BEHAVIORAL DEFINITIONS

1. Intelligence level less than 70 on an individually administered, standardized test of mental ability.
2. Lacks daily living skills necessary to adapt to the cultural community.
3. Expressive-only or receptive and expressive language delays and/or deficits.
4. Delayed and/or disordered phonological development.
5. Difficulty with social communication in the home, school, community or vocational setting.

___. _____

_____

___. _____

_____

_____

___. _____

_____

LONG-TERM GOALS

1. Communicate needs and wants in daily routine situations.
2. Increase awareness and discrimination of different stimuli.
3. Use key vocabulary in daily communication.
4. Use conventional morphology and syntax during interactions with others.
5. Use appropriate social pragmatic communication in interactions with others.
6. Use conversational phonological skills commensurate with mental abilities.

7. Use augmentative/alternative communication to interact effectively with others in daily routines.

—. _____

_____

—. _____

_____

—. _____

_____

SHORT-TERM OBJECTIVES

1. Participate willingly in a speech and language assessment. (1, 2, 3, 4, 5)

THERAPEUTIC INTERVENTIONS

1. Administer standardized speech-language tests (if not mental ability age-appropriate, adapt standardized tests and use as a criterion-referenced assessment) to determine the client's overall speech-language strengths and weaknesses and to compare his/her speech-language development to dialectal, cultural, and developmental norms.

2. Administer criterion-referenced tests to determine the client's specific speech-language strengths and weaknesses.

3. Videotape a communication sample that represents the client's typical means of communication while engaged in his/her favorite routine activity that requires interaction; analyze the sample for the client's communication (e.g., preintentional, intentional, gestural, augmentative/alternative, or verbal interactions with others).

4. Interview the client's parents, teacher, classroom aide, the

2. Cooperate with an oral-motor examination. (6)

3. Participate willingly in an audiological evaluation. (7)

4. Parents participate in the evaluation process and contribute to the interpretation of evaluation information. (8, 9)

client, if appropriate, and other relevant academic professionals to determine his/her social and academic strengths and weaknesses.

5. Assess the client's communicative skills in the classroom, playground, cafeteria, vocational, community, or other critical social and academic situations.

6. Evaluate the client's oral-motor skills by first observing the visible structure of his/her face, lips, teeth, tongue, hard and soft palate and then assess how he/she uses specific structures important for speech and language production (e.g., movement, strength, and closure of the lips; strength, protrusion, retraction, and lateralization of the tongue; or movement of the soft palate when producing the /a/ phoneme).

7. Conduct a pure-tone audiological screening at 500 Hz, 1000 Hz, 2000 Hz, and 4000 Hz at 20 dB if the client is able to respond reliably; refer him/her to an audiologist for a complete evaluation if the screening cannot be completed or if results of the audiological screening indicate a need for further assessment.

8. Ask the parents to provide information on the client's developmental milestones, current medical status and history, previous professional intervention, communicative attempts in different settings,

and relevant social and family concerns.

9. Parents seek a medical evaluation for the client from a pediatrician or an otolaryngologist (ear/nose/throat physician) if indicated to identify any organic bases for the speech-language disorder.

5. Parents accept the recommendations given and collaboratively select language targets and a general intervention strategy. (10, 11, 12)

10. Conduct a meeting with the parents and other professionals, first, to determine the client's eligibility for services, second, to develop collaborative intervention strategies, and, third, to determine the most appropriate therapeutic approach (e.g., collaborative or consultative) for his/her individual needs.

11. Collaboratively select daily routines for focusing on speech and language goals with the client's parents and teachers.

12. Select specific vocabulary, word/sentence structures, and/or pragmatic situations as targets for intervention based on the client's mental abilities; chronological age; phonological skills; motor skills; speech intelligibility; dialect; and social, vocational, and/or academic communicative needs.

6. Parents accept the client's speech and language deficits relative to his/her developmental and physical status, develop realistic expectations, and look for positive and supportive resources. (13, 14)

13. Explain to the client's parents, teachers, and other relevant professionals the relationships among speech and language development and age, cognition, mental abilities, and physical status.

14. Provide helpful references and resources on mental impair-

7. Parents and teachers work to include the client in mainstream educational and recreational activities with typically developing peers. (15, 16)

8. Parents, teachers, and significant others identify the communicative intentions of the client's unconventional means of communication. (17, 18)

ment and communication disorders for the client's parents and teachers (see the American Association on Mental Retardation at http://www.aamr.org).

15. Help parents and teachers advocate for education-based resources (e.g., instructional paraprofessional aides and curriculum adaptations) to enable the client to be included successfully in classrooms with age-appropriate typically developing peers.

16. Assist the client in developing a circle-of-friends group that includes activities such as the client and typically developing peers meeting for recreational activities during lunch hours and after school.

17. Examine what the client does immediately before and after tantrums, self-stimulating behavior, or aggressive acts to determine whether he/she is communicating desires or demands, need for attention, or the need to escape.

18. Help the client's parents learn to recognize his/her nonverbal signals and unconventional communicative attempts (e.g., smelling and/or touching peers, grinding teeth, or grabbing desired objects) and then help the parents model conventional ways of communicating for the client during or immediately after his/her unconventional attempt.

9. Increase the length of eye contact or joint attention. (19, 20)

10. Expand the frequency and range of conventional intentional communication. (21, 22, 23)

19. Encourage the client to establish eye contact with you before giving him/her a desired object or a favorite food; reinforce eye contact when it is given.

20. Use engaging toys that make sounds or movements or audio players with music; wait for the client to establish eye contact with you or the toy and then start the toy or music; when he/she turns his/her attention elsewhere, turn the toy or music off and then turn it back on when the client again establishes joint attention.

21. Arrange age-appropriate, desired objects slightly out of reach so that the client must protest or request the objects by using eye gaze, reaching movements, and/or vocalizations; reinforce these attempts to communicate.

22. Change routine interactions in a surprising manner (e.g., first giving the client blocks one at a time to put in a can and then surreptitiously giving him/her a different small toy instead of a block or put client-desired objects in see-through containers that are difficult for him/her to open); model the appropriate communication intention for the client (e.g., using eye gaze, reaching movements, and/or vocalizations); ensure that objects/toys are age-appropriate.

23. Provide multiple opportunities for the client to make verbal or nonverbal choices throughout his/her daily routines (e.g., "Would you like to listen to

music or a story?" or "Do you want cottage cheese or apple sauce?"); reinforce any communication of choice.

11. Use symbolic skills during interactions with others. (24, 25, 26)

24. Model and reinforce the client when imitating actions needed for daily living skills (e.g., washing face, combing hair, or brushing teeth).

25. Use modeling and contingent reinforcement to teach the client to match pictures of objects to corresponding real objects.

26. Teach the child to understand and use the Picture Exchange System (PECS) by Bondy and Frost or basic sign language to communicate needs and wants.

12. Implement the use of key vocabulary needed for communication in the home, school, community, and/or vocational settings with 80% accuracy. (27, 28)

27. Teach the client's parents strategies to expose him/her to new vocabulary during daily activities in different settings (e.g., extending his/her utterance with additional semantic information, recasting his/her utterance into a different type of utterance, or parallel talk, which is providing the utterances for him/her during an activity).

28. First, ask the client to point to pictures or objects that represent a word; then ask him/her to imitate your production of the words; and, finally, prompt him/her to use the new vocabulary in different daily routines.

13. Use augmentative/alternative communication to communicate with others. (29)

29. Teach the client to use augmentative/alternative communication to interact effectively in everyday situations (see Augmentative/

Alternative Communication chapter in this *Planner* for specific interventions).

14. Engage in conversations about past and future familiar events. (30, 31)

30. Instruct the client's parents to discuss past and future events in the client's life as part of their daily interactions by using pictures of him/her participating in different significant activities (e.g., birthday parties, vacations, or holidays).

31. Make a daily routine picture book that chronicles the client's activities throughout the day; teach him/her to describe what he/she did and what he/she will do in the future.

15. Increase utterance length to communicate more meaningful information. (32)

32. Teach client's parents and teachers to use communicative strategies that model and encourage increased utterance length (e.g., *expansion:* saying a more mature version of his/her previous utterance, *turnabout:* acknowledging his/her previous utterance and then asking a question that extends the current topic, or *contingent query:* asking the client to repeat or clarify what he/she just said).

16. Improve speech sound production to 80% accuracy. (33)

33. Teach the client to use conventional phonological skills that enable him/her to interact effectively in everyday situations (see Phonological Disorders chapter in this *Planner* for specific interventions).

17. Develop literacy skills needed for daily communication at school, work, and in the home. (34, 35)

34. Encourage the client's parents to engage in preliteracy activities (e.g., routinely reading to the client), discussing print in his/her environment, providing

access to writing materials, and providing multiple experiences with sounds (e.g., rhyming games or preliteracy computer programs).

35. Teach the client specific vocabulary that he/she needs for survival in the community (e.g., street signs, menus, store names), for his/her vocation, or for his/her augmentative communication device.

18. Use appropriate social communication in work and community settings. (36, 37)

36. Role-play ways of initiating and responding to others with the client (e.g., polite greetings, introductions, and requests appropriate for various situations and/or conversational partners); monitor and redirect his/her social communication in the actual situations (e.g., ordering a cup of hot chocolate, going to a basketball game, or asking a question on the job).

37. First help the client to recognize when he/she does not understand and then teach him/her strategies (e.g., saying "What?," "I don't understand," or "Wait a minute") for requesting others to clarify the misunderstanding in conversations in various situations.

—. _____

_____

—. _____

_____

—. _____

_____

—. _____

_____

—. _____

_____

—. _____

_____

DIAGNOSTIC SUGGESTIONS:

Axis I: 317   Mild Mental Retardation
                318.0   Moderate Mental Retardation
                318.1   Severe Mental Retardation
                318.2   Profound Mental Retardation
                319   Mental Retardation, Severity Unspecified

_____   _____

_____   _____

PERVASIVE DEVELOPMENTAL DISORDER—ASPERGER'S SYNDROME

BEHAVIORAL DEFINITIONS

1. Consistent and significant deficits with social interaction.
2. Difficulty with use of eye contact, facial expressions, gestures, and other forms of nonverbal communication.
3. Difficulty with understanding and using nonliteral language.
4. Lack of appropriate peer relationships.
5. Rigid preoccupations with interests or objects.
6. Rigid adherence to routines or specific interests that interferes with engaging in communicative activities.

—. _____

_____

—. _____

_____

—. _____

_____

LONG-TERM GOALS

1. Attend to communicative verbal and nonverbal acts.
2. Initiate and to respond to social interactions with others.
3. Understand and use figurative language to communicate effectively.
4. Accept and manage variations in everyday routines without strong emotional reaction.
5. Develop social interaction skills appropriate for developmental age, dialect, and cultural expectations in various communicative contexts.

6. Parents establish realistic expectations for their child's communicative skills and work collaboratively with the speech-language pathologist (SLP) and other professionals to develop effective treatment strategies.

__. _____
   _____
__. _____
   _____
__. _____
   _____

SHORT-TERM OBJECTIVES

1. Parents and others in the client's home and community environment participate willingly in a communication assessment of the client. (1, 2, 3)

THERAPEUTIC INTERVENTIONS

1. Document the client's communicative skills by using standardized assessments (e.g., Preschool Language Scale-IV, Oral-Written Language Scales, or Test of Pragmatic Language) and making observations of his/her communication in the home, classroom, playground, cafeteria, and other critical social and academic situations.

2. Ask the parents to provide information on the client's developmental milestones, current medical status and history, previous professional intervention, communicative attempts in different settings, and social and family concerns.

3. Advise the parents to seek a transdisciplinary evaluation for the client from relevant professionals (e.g., educational psychologist, teacher, pediatric neurologist, occupational therapist, or audiologist) to document the cognitive,

2. Parents contribute to the interpretation of evaluation information. (4)

3. Parents accept the recommendations developed and collaboratively select communicative behavioral goals for the client. (5, 6)

4. Parents and teachers develop realistic expectations for the client and look for positive and supportive resources. (7, 8)

5. Parents, teachers, and, if appropriate, the client identify and implement appropriate environmental

educational, health, hearing, daily living, and motor skills important for developing appropriate communicative interventions.

4. Conduct regular meetings with the client's parents and other relevant professionals to develop and change collaborative intervention strategies, as needed.

5. Determine the most appropriate therapeutic approaches for the client's individual needs (e.g., floor time, Treatment and Education of Autistic and related Communication handicapped CHildren [TEACCH] model, social stories, and/or social-pragmatic approaches).

6. Select specific communicative situations as targets for intervention for the client based on his/her linguistic, social, and academic communicative needs.

7. Explain to the client's parents, teachers, and other relevant professionals the relationships between behaviors related to autism and communication development deficits.

8. Provide helpful references and resources on Asperger's syndrome for the client's parents and teachers (see the Autism Society of America at http://www.autism-society.org or http://www.asperger.net).

9. Explore environmental supports that are needed to maximize the client's communicative success with the client's parents and

supports that enhance the client's social interaction with family members, teachers, and peers. (9)

6. Parents and teachers verbalize an understanding of the client's need for consistent and routine activities and help to develop communicative systems for managing changes in his/her daily activities. (10, 11)

7. Engage in joint action routines with adults and peers. (12, 13)

teachers (e.g., posting daily schedules at home and at school, providing written rules for participating in games or learning centers, removing overwhelming sensory materials, or managing noise levels).

10. When explaining variations in the client's schedule, instruct the parents and teachers to use visual supports (e.g., posting the word "change" or symbols that indicate disruptions in his/her daily schedule); ask the client to verbalize the change in his/her daily schedule.

11. Provide a visual story for him/her that consists of a visual if-then map that first has a picture representing an "If this happens . . ." event and also has two or three pictures of "Then I can use . . ." alternative communicative behaviors (e.g., "If I get angry with another student, then I can move away from him or I can tell the student why I am angry with a calm and quiet voice").

12. When engaged in an activity with the client, describe his/her actions and your actions while using a melodic tone of voice with a slower speech rate and exaggerated facial expressions to provide more salience.

13. Determine meaningful verbal and nonverbal communicative behaviors that the client needs to use for specific joint action or cooperative interaction routines (e.g., preparing a meal, playing a game or sports, going to the store, or ordering in a restaurant)

then prepare a script of the facial expressions, body language, phrases, and sentence structures that he/she should use; after modeling the appropriate communication, have him/her practice the appropriate communication with typically developing peers during the joint action routine.

8. Follow oral instructions for specific tasks with 80% accuracy. (14, 15, 16)

14. Limit oral directions for the client to one directive while using simple gestures and facial expressions to enhance the verbal information; provide adequate time for him/her to respond and indicate that he/she has correctly comprehended the direction.

15. Add visual cues (e.g., written or symbolic pictures) for oral directions by making story boards of each explicit step in a task; ask the client to read the directions before beginning the task (e.g., handing out snacks in a preschool room, completing an assignment, putting personal items in his/her locker, or setting the table).

16. Model the steps of a task for the client when providing specific oral instructions before asking him/her to follow your oral directions; for each task, ask him/her to repeat your oral direction, adding more complex sequential tasks over time as the client increases his/her ability to attend for longer periods of time.

9. Verbalize an accurate interpretation of others' emotions, feelings, and

17. Use pictures of people with different facial expressions and body positions to teach the client

points of view based on their verbal and nonverbal messages. (17, 18, 19)

the common meanings of nonverbal communicative messages.

18. Instruct the client's parents and teachers to comment frequently on the verbal and nonverbal behaviors of significant others that indicate feelings and emotions (e.g., "Look at Jim's face. His face looks sad because Mary said something that hurt his feelings. Do you see that?" or "Look at Mark! He is smiling and jumping up and down. He's excited because he got a good grade on his paper.").

19. After reading stories and viewing movies with the client, discuss characters' feelings and emotions; ask him/her to draw or write responses to complete the following sentences: "When this happened, ____ felt ____. I know this because he/she ____."

10. Gain another person's attention appropriately. (20)

20. Teach the client how to get another person's attention appropriately by saying his/her name, lightly tapping the person on the shoulder, or saying opening phrases (e.g., "You know what?"); teach the client to wait until the person has acknowledged his/her attempt by looking at or responding to him/her with the question: "What?"

11. Engage in more than three conversational turns on the same topic with appropriate verbal and nonverbal communication. (21, 22, 23)

21. Teach the client to reduce his/her interruptions of a speaker during conversations by identifying changes in the speaker's eye gaze and use of pauses that allow the client to

take a turn at the appropriate conversational moment.

22. Provide a list of common contingent questions that the client can use to continue a topic (e.g., "What happened next?" or "What did you do?") in conversations with peers and adults; teach him/her how to ask contingent questions when listening to another person tell a personal story, making sure that he/she knows how to wait for the speaker to pause before asking the question.

23. Teach the client to use verbal (e.g., "really?" or "mhmm") and nonverbal acknowledgements (e.g., smiles, frowns, head nods) at appropriate times in conversations with others.

12. Use questions to initiate conversations appropriately with others. (24, 25)

24. Teach the client to use questions (e.g., "Can I play?") to initiate social interactions instead of using inappropriate nonverbal behavior (e.g., pushing others or taking toys without permission).

25. Make a list of questions that the client can use to get information from others (e.g., "Would you like to play?" "What did you do on your vacation?" or "What are you going to do this weekend?") and then teach him/her how to use these questions to begin conversations with others.

13. Make at least one change in topic during conversations with others. (26, 27)

26. Teach the client to move from engaging in monologues to dialogues on a favorite topic by providing him/her with key questions or comments (e.g., "Do you know what I mean?"

"Have you ever . . . ?") or a sequence of questions (e.g., "Did you see that movie too? Did you like it when _____?") to use for inviting others to take turns in the conversation.

27. Provide the client with comic strip conversations that illustrate rules for maintaining conversations with others (e.g., requesting or responding to requests for clarification, giving signals for topic shifts, providing too much or too little information, and smoothly ending a topic in a conversation); keep the comic strips in a notebook for the client to review as needed.

14. Engage in appropriate social interactions in various situations with different conversational partners. (28, 29, 30)

28. Arrange social clubs for the client with typically developing peers that center on his/her special interests (e.g., playing computer games, playing chess, or conducting scientific experiments); use this time to videotape him/her and to discuss appropriate and inappropriate social interactions with peers.

29. With the client, write social story scripts that are directly related to his/her regular activities, which outline the individual parts of an activity and the expected types of social communication necessary in school, home, and community situations; ask him/her to read or listen to audio recordings of the social story scripts every day before engaging in the activities. (For additional strategies, see *The New Social Story Book* by Carol Gray.)

30. Divide a group of students, including the client and his/her typically developing peers, into two teams and play "What happens next?"; first, present a problematic social situation; second, ask each team to think of at least three different ways of solving the situation by stating what the persons should say and do next (e.g., "Mary wants to go to a party tonight, but her father is still upset that she stayed out past her curfew last week. What could Mary do and say in this situation?"); third, ask the students to role-play the problem and solutions; and fourth, ask the students to decide which solution is the best and why.

15. Demonstrate an understanding of developmentally appropriate abstract language with 80% accuracy. (31, 32)

31. Instruct the client to illustrate the figurative meanings of idioms, metaphors, or similes (e.g., "letting the cat out of the bag," "as the crow flies," "bull-headed," or "as free as a bird"); ask him/her to say or write sentences that include the definition or use of the idioms.

32. Using comic strips, cartoons, newspaper headlines, and jokes, help the client understand figurative language that includes multiple meanings (e.g., "tip" the waiter or "tip" of a pencil), sarcasm (e.g., "aren't you the picture of cleanliness!"), and dual-meaning headlines (new autos to hit five million); then teach the client to share his/her favorite type of humor, to use sarcasm, or to create headlines in a socially acceptable manner.

16. Tell jokes appropriately to peers. (32)

32. Using comic strips, cartoons, newspaper headlines, and jokes, help the client understand figurative language that includes multiple meanings (e.g., "tip" the waiter or "tip" of a pencil), sarcasm (e.g., "aren't you the picture of cleanliness!"), and dual-meaning headlines (new autos to hit five million); then teach the client to share his/her favorite type of humor, to use sarcasm, or to create headlines in a socially acceptable manner.

—. _____   —. _____
   _____   _____
—. _____   —. _____
   _____   _____
—. _____   —. _____
   _____   _____

DIAGNOSTIC SUGGESTIONS:

Axis I: 299.80   Asperger's Disorder
              299.80   Pervasive Developmental Disorder NOS

              _____   _____
              _____   _____

PERVASIVE DEVELOPMENTAL DISORDER—AUTISM

BEHAVIORAL DEFINITIONS

1. Delayed and/or abnormal development in communication with others.
2. Loss of language usually reported between the ages of 18 to 36 months.
3. Consistent and significant deficits with social interaction.
4. Lack of symbolic and imaginative play.
5. Delayed and/or immediate repetition of words or phrases.
6. Rigid adherence to routines that interferes with engaging in communicative activities.

—. _____
   _____

—. _____
   _____

—. _____
   _____

LONG-TERM GOALS

1. Attend to communicative verbal and nonverbal acts.
2. Initiate and respond to social interactions with others.
3. Understand and use language to communicate effectively.
4. Accept and manage variations in everyday routines without strong emotional reaction.
5. Develop social interaction skills appropriate for developmental age, dialect, and cultural expectations in various communicative contexts.

6. Parents establish realistic expectations for their child's communicative skills and work collaboratively with the speech-language pathologist (SLP) and other professionals to develop effective treatment strategies.

—. _____

 _____

—. _____

 _____

—. _____

 _____

SHORT-TERM OBJECTIVES

1. Parents and others in the client's home and community environment participate willingly in a communication assessment of the client. (1, 2, 3)

THERAPEUTIC INTERVENTIONS

1. Document the client's communicative skills in the home, classroom, playground, cafeteria, or other critical social and academic situations using observational instruments (e.g., Communication and Symbolic Behavior Scales by Wetherby and Prizant and Functional Emotional Assessment Scale by Greenspan).

2. Ask the parents to provide information on the client's developmental milestones, current medical status and history, previous professional intervention, communicative attempts in different settings, and relevant social and family concerns.

3. Advise the parents to seek a transdisciplinary evaluation for the client from relevant professionals (e.g., an educational psychologist, teacher, pediatric neurologist, occupational therapist, and/or audiologist) to obtain information regarding

2. Parents contribute to the interpretation of evaluation information. (4)

3. Parents accept the recommendations developed and collaboratively select communicative behavioral goals for the client. (5, 6)

4. Parents and teachers accept the client's communicative deficits relative to his/her developmental, cognitive, and physical status of the client, develop realistic expectations and look for positive and supportive resources. (7, 8)

cognitive, educational, health, hearing, daily living, and motor skills important for developing appropriate communication interventions.

4. Conduct a meeting with the parents and, if needed, other relevant professionals, first, to determine the client's eligibility for services and, second, to develop collaborative intervention strategies.

5. Determine the most appropriate therapeutic approaches for the client's individual needs (e.g., floor time, prelinguistic milieu teaching, Treatment and Education of Autistic and related Communication handicapped CHildren [TEACCH] model).

6. Select specific communicative intentions, vocabulary, or communicative situations as targets for intervention based on the client's developmental age, cognitive ability, motor skills, and social and academic communicative needs.

7. Explain to the client's parents, teachers, and other relevant professionals the relationships between behaviors related to autism and communication development deficits.

8. Provide helpful references and resources on autism and communication development for the client's parents and teachers (e.g., *More Than Words* by Sussman or the Autism Society of America at http://www.autism-society.org).

5. Parents, teachers, and, if appropriate, the client identify positive communicative consequences that may be used to reinforce progress. (9)

6. Parents and teachers verbalize an understanding of the client's use of immediate and delayed echolalia to communicate. (10)

7. Reduce perseverative activities to become more intentionally communicative. (11)

8. Use prelinguistic intentional communication to meet immediate needs at least two times per day. (12, 13)

9. Explore positive intrinsic reinforcers (e.g., receiving an immediate response to a clearly verbalized request or receiving a desired object after completing a clear communicative request) and extrinsic reinforcers (e.g., praise, stickers, small candy) that may be used to reinforce the client's successful communicative attempts with the client's parents and teachers.

10. Explain to the client's parents and teacher how linguistic and cognitive growth is related to the increased communicative functions of echolalia and then help his/her parents and teachers to become aware of the client's specific use of echolalia to communicate.

11. Teach the client's parents to playfully interrupt a perseverative activity by quietly pointing to or touching the object the client is playing with or gently blocking his/her next move (e.g., putting your hand in the spot he/she will place the next train car in a column) and then show the client's parents how to wait for a response, which may be as subtle as the client stopping and looking at the object.

12. Teach the client's parents and teachers to follow the child's lead in daily activities by commenting on what he/she does (e.g., "You put the red block next in line") or on how the child reacts to changes in the environment ("That truck made a loud noise").

13. Teach the client's parents and teachers to model prelinguistic communicative activities frequently, such as conventional gestures (e.g., reaching to get something out of reach, pointing to people or objects, shaking or nodding head) during common everyday situations.

9. Engage in activities that require joint attention with another person. (14, 15)

14. Instruct the client's parents to engage in parallel play with the client by doing the same play activity as the client but in a slightly different manner (e.g., if he/she is moving a toy car, the parent sits next to him/her and moves another car faster or slower than the client) and then teach the parents to look for the child to adjust his activity to match the parent's (e.g., the client also begins to move the car faster or slower) and, finally, to verbalize those changes (e.g., saying "fast" and "slow").

15. Teach the client's parents to pause while playing, singing, or playing routine games (e.g., Peek-a-Boo or riding horsie on the parent's knees) and then to recognize the client's body movements that communicate his/her desire to continue the activity by subtle movements (e.g., wiggling, pulling on the parent's arms, or looking at the parent; see *More Than Words* by Sussman).

10. Replace challenging behaviors with meaningful communication. (16, 17)

16. Teach the client's parents and teachers to determine the communicative function of the client's challenging behaviors (e.g., tantrums, head banging, or injuring self and others),

then help them learn to predict the behaviors' antecedents and, finally, teach the client's family and teachers to help the client say or nonverbally indicate key words (e.g., "no," "want," "more," and "yes") in place of challenging behaviors (see *Understanding and Intervening with Young Children's Problem Behaviors* by Fox, Dunlap, and Buschbacher).

17. If client's challenging behaviors are related to difficulty with transitions to new activities, make a visual schedule for the client that can be used to indicate the activities for the day and then help him/her use the schedule to choose activities and become accustomed to appropriate limits on challenging behaviors.

11. Exchange pictures or photos of desired objects or activities at least twice per day. (18)

18. Help the client learn to give photos or symbolic picture systems to communicate needs and desires, such as wanting to eat particular foods, play with toys, or do other routine activities.

12. Use questions to initiate conversations with others. (19, 20, 21)

19. Teach the client to say, "What's that?" when showing him/her highly desirable toys or food in a slightly opaque container; when he/she successfully imitates or independently produces the question, open the container and give the object to the client while clearly stating the name of the object.

20. Teach the client to say, "Where is it?" or "Where's ____?" after first showing and then hiding a favorite object in various key

locations (e.g., under a table, in a box, or behind the bookshelf).

21. Prompt the client to say, "Whose is it?" when showing objects that belong to him/her or other members of the family.

13. Use developmentally appropriate vocabulary to communicate intentionally with others. (22, 23)

22. After the client successfully imitates or independently asks what or where an object is, show him/her the object and state its label and location and then wait expectantly for him/her to imitate the label.

23. During common routine activities, teach the client's parents to model age-appropriate vocabulary frequently and then to wait expectantly for the client to imitate the modeled vocabulary in those situations.

14. Demonstrate developmentally and age-appropriate symbolic play behaviors at least once per day. (24)

24. Provide the client with communicative and behavioral scripts for participating in developmentally appropriate play situations (e.g., pretending to have a tea party or having a birthday party) by setting up regular play times with typically developing peers and then coaching him/her through the play activity with models and verbal and nonverbal prompts.

15. Engage in appropriate social interactions appropriately in various situations with different conversational partners. (25, 26)

25. Model communicative routines (e.g., how to make introductions, greetings, or get someone's attention, clarify misunderstandings, and knowing when to speak and when to be quiet) that are typical situations for the client.

26. With the client, write social story scripts, which are directly related to his/her regular activities, that

outline the individual parts of an activity and the expected types of social communication necessary in school, home, and community situations then ask the client to read or listen to audio recordings of the social story scripts every day before engaging in the activities (for specific social stories, see *The New Social Story Book* by Carol Gray).

16. Attend to visual, auditory, or kinesthetic sensations in the environment while remaining calm up to 90% of the day. (27, 28)

27. In collaboration with an occupational therapist, provide sensory integration intervention to reduce sensory hyperactivity or hypoactivity and then encourage the client to plan, communicate, and implement appropriate adaptive behaviors for coping with sensory input.

28. Write and regularly practice scripts with the client for alternative verbal reactions to predictable visual, auditory, or kinesthetic input (e.g., reacting to the recess bell in school by verbalizing that it is recess time rather than screaming).

17. Develop an understanding of developmentally appropriate abstract language with 80% accuracy. (29)

29. Teach the client the meanings of more abstract mental state verbs (e.g., "love," "think," or "hope") through role-playing with typically developing peers in real-life situations.

__. _____

_____

__. _____

_____

__. _____

_____

__. _____

_____

__. _____

_____

__. _____

_____

DIAGNOSTIC SUGGESTIONS:

Axis I: 299.00   Autistic Disorder
                299.80   Pervasive Developmental Disorder NOS

_____   _____

_____   _____

PHONOLOGICAL DISORDERS

BEHAVIORAL DEFINITIONS

1. Overall phonological production is substantially below expected phonological developmental norms.
2. Consistent and significant difficulty producing phonemes in different positions within words, phrases, and/or sentences.
3. Spontaneous speech is consistently judged to be unintelligible by unfamiliar adults.
4. Production of phonemes in conversations interferes significantly with effective communication at home, school, and community.
5. Significant deficit in the awareness of phonological linguistic features, which in turn affects speech production.
6. Consistent and significant difficulty with the oral-motor strength and/ or movement needed for the respiration, phonation, resonation, and articulation aspects of speech production.

—. _____
   _____

—. _____
   _____

—. _____
   _____

LONG-TERM GOALS

1. Produce phonemes in different communicative contexts appropriate for age, cognition, physical ability, and dialect.
2. Clear intelligibility when communicating with others at home, school, and in the community.

3. Develop understanding of the phonological features of language.
4. Increase oral-motor skills, leading to improved speech production.
5. Develop awareness of phonological deficits and work to overcome or use compensatory strategies for those deficits.
6. Parents establish realistic expectations for their child's phonological skills and work collaboratively with the speech-language pathologist (SLP) to develop effective treatment strategies.

—. _____
   _____
   _____

—. _____
   _____
   _____

—. _____
   _____

SHORT-TERM OBJECTIVES

1. Participate willingly in a phonological assessment. (1, 2, 3, 4)

THERAPEUTIC INTERVENTIONS

1. Administer an articulation test to determine the client's phoneme production in initial, medial, and final positions of words and in connected speech, to assess his/her stimulability for error phonemes, and to compare his/her phonological development to dialect and developmental norms.

2. Administer a phonological processes test to evaluate the client's error patterns (e.g., final-consonant deletion, initial-consonant deletion, cluster simplification, velar fronting, gliding, depalatization, deaffrication, or fronting).

3. Videotape a conversational speech sample that represents the client's typical connected speech production while playing with interactive toys or

discussing favorite television shows, movies, books, or games; analyze the tape for his/her phonological production.

4. Establish a measurable baseline of the client's phonological skills before treatment begins.

2. Cooperate with an oral-motor examination. (5)

5. Evaluate the client's oral-motor skills by first observing the visible structure of his/her face, lips, teeth, tongue, and hard and soft palate and then assess how he/she uses specific structures important for speech production (e.g., movement, strength, and closure of the lips; strength, protrusion, retraction, and lateralization of the tongue; or movement of the soft palate when producing the /a/ phoneme).

3. Participate willingly in an audiological evaluation. (6, 7)

6. Conduct a pure-tone audiological screening at 500 Hz, 1000 Hz, 2000 Hz, and 4000 Hz at 20 dB for children and 25 dB for adults.

7. Refer the client to an audiologist for a complete evaluation if results of the audiological screening indicate a need for further assessment.

4. Parents and the client, if age-appropriate, participate in the evaluation process and contribute to the interpretation of evaluation information. (8, 9)

8. Ask the parents and the client, if age-appropriate, to provide information on his/her developmental milestones, current medical status and history, previous professional intervention, phonological production in the home, and relevant social and family concerns.

9. Encourage the parents to seek a medical evaluation from an

5. Parents and the client, if age-appropriate, accept the recommendations given and collaboratively select phonological targets and a general intervention strategy. (10, 11, 12)

6. Parents accept their child's phonological deficits relative to the developmental, cognitive and physical status of their child, develop realistic expectations, and look for positive and supportive resources. (13, 14, 15)

otolaryngologist (ear/nose/throat physician), if indicated, to identify any organic bases for the client's phonological disorder.

10. Conduct a meeting with the parents and the client, if age-appropriate, first, to determine his/her eligibility for services and, second, to develop collaborative intervention strategies.

11. Determine the most appropriate general therapeutic approach (i.e., linguistic-based or motor-based) for the client's individual needs.

12. Select specific phonemes or phonological processes as targets for intervention based on the child's age, stimulability, intelligibility, dialect, and/or social and educational communicative needs.

13. Explain to the parents the relationships between phonological development and age, cognition, and physical status.

14. Provide helpful references and resources on phonological disorders for the parents (see Internet resources from the American Speech-Language-Hearing Association at http://www.asha.org).

15. Introduce the client's parents to other parents of children with phonological disorders for informal support or for facilitating their participation in a local support group.

7. Identify consequences that may be used to reinforce phonological production progress. (16)

8. Verbalize an understanding of how specific therapeutic interventions contribute to better phonological skills and how these skills ultimately lead to effective communication. (17, 18)

9. Increase intelligibility to 80% by reducing phono-logical processes, as judged by the SLP. (19)

10. Parents take an active role in working positively with their

16. Explore what consequences may be used to reinforce the client's successful phonological attempts positively (e.g., extrinsic reinforcers, such as food, stickers, and other tokens or verbal praise and intrinsic reinforcers, such as receiving an immediate response to a clearly verbalized request).

17. Before beginning an activity, clearly state the therapeutic goal of the activity for the client (e.g., "We are using the mirror to help you learn how to make the /s/ sound") and, again, at the end of the activity, ask him/her to tell you the specific goal for that activity.

18. Help the client chart therapeutic progress by indicating phonological accomplishments on a visual aid illustrating the sequential stages necessary for achieving long-term goals.

19. If the client is highly unintelligible, select a cycles-intervention approach to target identified phonological processes: (1) read a word list with amplification that highlights specific phonological processes used by the client, (2) ask the client to color and paste three to five pictures of carefully selected words, (3) help the client say the words on the picture cards, (4) assess the client's stimulability for other phonemes, and (5) read the same word list again.

20. Maintain ongoing, frequent con-tact with the parents, discussing

child on daily 10-minute phonological exercises. (20, 21, 22)

11. Increase the oral-motor strength and movement needed to produce the desired phonemes in connected speech. (23)

12. Discriminate correctly between contrasting target phonemes in minimal pair words with 90% accuracy. (24, 25, 26)

specific methods for eliciting phonological productions and reporting progress or concerns regarding the client's phono-logical needs.

21. Ask the parents to read lists of 10 to 12 words to the client every day that contain specific phonemes that illustrate his/her targeted phonological processes.

22. After each therapy session, pro-vide worksheets or picture cards of five to ten target phonemes, words, or phrases for the client to practice daily at home under parental supervision.

23. Assign the client to practice specific oral-motor exercises to be used in combination with speech tasks (e.g., doing tongue lifts to the alveolar ridge while making placements for the /l/ sound) for five to ten minutes per day to increase the strength and control of muscles needed for speech production.

24. Instruct the client to choose the pictures that represent the words he/she hears when shown pictures of minimal pair words (e.g., "me" or "meet") that high-light his/her target phonemes (e.g., /t/ and /k/ or /w/ and /r/) or phonological processes.

25. Teach the client to sort contrasting word cards into categories of his/her target phonemes and other categories of nontarget phonemes.

26. Assist the client in determining whether target sounds occur in the initial prevocalic, medial

intervocalic, or final postvocalic positions of words (e.g., ask if the /l/ sound in yellow is in the beginning, middle, or end of the word).

13. Discriminate between correct and incorrect productions of phonemes with 90% accuracy. (27, 28)

27. Say the client's incorrect patterns of speech production purposefully on some of the words in a familiar short story and instruct him/her to listen carefully and say, "I heard it!" after hearing the incorrect production.

28. When viewing video recordings of the client practicing intervention strategies, ask the client to identify his/her correct and incorrect phonological productions.

14. Make the correct articulatory placement for target phonemes. (29, 30, 31)

29. Use mirrors and tongue blades or cotton swab sticks to provide detailed kinesthetic and visual cues to position the client's lips, teeth, and/or tongue for target phonemes.

30. Present pictures, diagrams, or computer simulations of the positions of the articulators to the client as models of the placement needed for specific phonemes.

31. Use phonemes with similar distinctive features to elicit target phonemes (e.g., ask the client to repeat the aspirated /t/ phoneme quickly to produce the /s/ phoneme); point out that the articulator positions are similar.

15. Imitate target phonemes correctly in isolation or in syllables with 90% accuracy, given an adult model. (32)

32. After instructing the client to listen carefully to a verbal model, ask him/her to imitate nonsense syllables of the target

phoneme in consonant-vowel, vowel-consonant, consonant-vowel-consonant, vowel-consonant-vowel, and consonant-vowel-consonant-vowel combinations.

16. Pronounce target phonemes correctly in words with 90% accuracy. (33, 34)

33. Provide practice on different phonetic contexts in words in a sequential manner: (1) the target phoneme in the initial prevocalic position, (2) in the final postvocalic position, (3) in the medial intervocalic position, (4) in blends, and (5) in all different positions of the word.

34. Provide practice on minimal contrast paired words (e.g., "see" and "seat" or "Sue" and "shoe") that target the client's phonological processes by asking the child to request certain items or to retell stories that use minimally contrasting pairs.

17. Pronounce target phonemes correctly in phrases and sentences with 80% accuracy. (35, 36)

35. Provide practice on target phonemes in phrases or short sentences by using slow-motion speech, echo speech, unison speaking, or role playing.

36. Have the client play games that require the use of target phonemes in phrases and/or sentences (e.g., given objects or word cards with the client's target phonemes, play barrier games, I Spy, or Twenty Questions using carrier phrases that contain target phonemes).

18. Pronounce target phonemes correctly during conversations with 80% accuracy. (37, 38, 39)

37. Have the client read or retell developmentally appropriate stories or jokes and riddles using correct phonological productions of the target phonemes.

38. Monitor and correct the client's speech production during conversations by asking leading questions: (1) "Tell me about your favorite movie or television show," (2) "How do you play baseball?," (3) "If you won a million dollars, what would you do?," or (4) "What did you do during your vacation?"

39. Role play different communicative situations (e.g., having a tea party, making a telephone call, or having a dinner conversation) for the client to practice target phonemes in conversational tasks; monitor and correct phonological production.

19. Pronounce target phonemes accurately and consistently in different communicative situations, as judged by the client's teachers, parents, and peers. (40)

40. Survey the client's parents, teachers, and significant others to determine whether he/she is using the target phonemes accurately in daily conversations.

—. _____

—. _____

—. _____

—. _____

—. _____

—. _____

DIAGNOSTIC SUGGESTIONS:

Axis I: 307.9   Communication Disorder NOS
             315.39   Phonological Disorder

_____   _____

_____   _____

RIGHT HEMISPHERE DYSFUNCTION

BEHAVIORAL DEFINITIONS

1. Hyperfluent, tangential, nonrelevant speech resulting in an inability to express a coherent narrative.
2. Concreteness of interpretation resulting in difficulty understanding jokes, proverbs, and abstract discourse.
3. Inability to maintain attention to persons or tasks.
4. Difficulties organizing and processing incoming auditory and written information.
5. Difficulties distinguishing trivial from salient stimuli.
6. Impulsivity and poor judgment resulting in poor safety awareness.
7. Denial of one's own illness.
8. Inattention to the left visual field and to the left side of the body.
9. Undue attention given to insignificant details.
10. Short-term memory problems.
11. Disorientation to persons, time, and the immediate environment.

__. _____
   _____

__. _____
   _____
   _____

__. _____
   _____

LONG-TERM GOALS

1. Demonstrate functional auditory and expressive integration skills by engaging effectively in connected discourse.

2. Consistently use compensatory strategies to improve orientation in time and the immediate environment and to aid memory.
3. The family structures the home environment in a way that maintains the client's orientation and memory skills.
4. The family develops realistic expectations regarding the client's cognitive and communication skills.

—. _____

_____

—. _____

_____

—. _____

_____

SHORT-TERM OBJECTIVES

1. Participate in a medical/ neurological evaluation. (1)

2. Participate in a speech-language evaluation. (2)

3. Participate with family/ caregivers in a meeting to learn the evaluation results and to agree on an intervention strategy. (3)

THERAPEUTIC INTERVENTIONS

1. Confer with the medical team about the client's current diagnosis, medical history, previous treatment, and rehabilitative potential.

2. Administer a speech/language evaluation focusing on the deficit areas involved in right-hemisphere disturbance (e.g., attention, orientation, perception, and verbal integration).

3. Arrange an interpretive staffing meeting with the client and his/ her family and caregivers to discuss the findings of the evaluation, the implications of the medical condition for speech and language, and the prognosis for recovery of functional communication skills; obtain information from the family on the client's level of education, occupation, and overall communicative sophistication to design

a treatment plan consistent with his/her communication needs.

4. Maintain consistent eye contact with other persons and stimulus materials. (4, 5)

4. Sitting in the client's visual field, manually move his/her head while giving the verbal cue, "Look at me" until eye contact is established, gradually fading the use of the physical prompt until he/she can maintain eye contact when given only a verbal or gestural cue; introduce other people to the session and have the client establish eye contact with them.

5. Place stimulus materials in the client's visual field and manually move his/her head while giving the verbal cue, "Look" until his/her gaze meets the materials; gradually fade the physical prompt until the client can fix his/her gaze on the task when given only a gestural or verbal cue.

5. Follow directives to demonstrate accurate scanning of printed material. (6, 7, 8)

6. Present the client with horizontal rows of large printed letters on a page; holding a pointer over the letters, well within his/her visual field, bring the client's visual attention to the left side of the page by instructing him/her to look at the pointer and follow it, reading each letter indicated by the pointer, while it is moved slowly to the left until reaching the final letter at the left margin.

7. Present the client with horizontal rows of large printed letters on a page; holding a pointer at the letter in the row where he/she first perceives the letters, have him/her read the letters

from that point, from right to left, to the end of the line; incrementally move the pointer to the left, repeating the process until the client directs his/her gaze all the way to the left margin.

8. Present the client with horizontal rows of large printed letters on a page; have him/her visually scan each row from left to right, circling letters as requested (e.g., circle all the "m's"); proceed from letters to words, then regular reading material.

6. Reduce extraneous, non-relevant verbalizations. (9, 10)

9. Agree with the client on a hand signal that the SLP will use (e.g., holding the hand up to indicate "Stop" or using the "Time Out" gesture) to indicate that the client's talking is rambling inappropriately; when the SLP gestures "Stop," the client stops talking and awaits redirection.

10. Play a tape-recorded sample of the client's spontaneous speech and have him/her note the digressions from the main topic.

7. Demonstrate appropriate conversational turn-taking skills. (11, 12)

11. Practice asking and answering questions using board games (e.g., Trivial Pursuit).

12. Conduct mock interviews in which the client asks the SLP about work, hobbies, and family; switch roles; guide him/her in the use of appropriate conversational exchange.

8. Convey the emotional content of speech by effective use of prosodic features. (13, 14)

13. Use modeling and behavior rehearsal to teach the client contrasting vocal intonation and rate patterns (e.g., interrogative ver-

sus declarative, serious versus sarcastic, enthusiastic versus bored, happy versus sad) that affect the emotional expression of speech.

14. Ask the client to label a written passage with stress marks and intonation patterns to indicate vocal expression; tape record him/her reading the passage and play it back; have the client critique the recording for effectiveness of expression.

9. Accurately identify significant others. (15)

15. Obtain photographs of the client's family and significant others, including hospital staff; label the photographs with each person's name and his/her relationship to the client; place these in a categorized notebook (e.g., "Family," "Friends," "Hospital Staff") and refer to the photographs when speaking to him/her about people.

10. Provide accurate information regarding time, date, and a simple schedule of activities. (16, 17, 18)

16. Encourage spontaneous use of a clock and watch by ensuring that the client has a clock with large numbers in his/her room and a wristwatch to wear; at intervals during the session, ask him/her to take note of the time, reinforcing accurate time perception.

17. Provide the client with a wall calendar for his/her room and with a pocket calendar to be carried; each day have him/her cross out the previous day's date on the calendar and direct him/her to the present date ("Yesterday was Wednesday the 10th. Today is Thursday the 11th"). Teach the client to refer

to the calendar at intervals to remind him/herself of the day.

18. Establish a schedule of daily activities with the client, including stipulation of the time, location, and people involved; rehearse the schedule with the client, cueing as necessary, and gradually fading the number of cues until he/she can use the schedule spontaneously or with minimal cues.

11. Accurately navigate around the living environment, including identifying and locating own room. (19, 20)

19. Have the client's family place many of his/her personal effects and familiar objects in his/her room; direct his/her attention to the objects, so he/she will be able to use them to identify the room as his/hers.

20. Familiarize the client with the residential environment by taking him/her on repeated walking tours of various areas in which he/she will be spending time, noting important landmarks (e.g., the nurses station, TV lounge, dining room) along the way to enhance memory; provide the client with a floor plan to be included in a pocket notebook. As the client's familiarity with the living environment increases, request him/her to show the way to a particular area or department using the previously learned landmarks as cues to lead him/her to the desired area.

12. Consistently use compensatory strategies to aid memory. (21, 22, 23, 24)

21. Develop a memory book for the client that includes personal identifying information, including the location of his/her

current residence, names of significant others, and a copy of his/her daily schedule; instruct the client's family and guests to make entries in the memory book, including the date and time of the visit, the people present, and the topics discussed.

22. Ask the client to recount previous visits with family and friends using the memory book, cueing him/her to use it as needed; gradually reduce the number of cues until the client can use the memory book spontaneously or with minimal cues.

23. Instruct the client in compensatory memory strategies (e.g., making "to do" lists, keeping files of important names, posting reminders in prominent places, and arranging immediate surroundings in a consistent, recognizable way).

24. Instruct the client in facilitative memory strategies (e.g., repetition, grouping information into meaningful units, focusing on the most meaningful information in a statement, using mnemonics).

13. Accurately write orally presented information. (25)

25. Organize a page using a grid format and then write letters and words in the squares for the client to copy; as his/her accuracy increases, eliminate the grid and dictate information for him/her to write (e.g., name and address), reinforcing accuracy and promptness in writing the information.

14. Accurately perform simple calculations. (26)

26. Have the client solve simple arithmetic problems; draw vertical lines on the paper to help the client keep numerical columns in proper order; expand calculation tasks to daily living problems (e.g., balancing a checkbook, making a purchase), reinforcing correctness of answers and promptness in solving the problems.

15. Correctly sequence activities of daily living. (27, 28)

27. Give the client written tasks that present an activity involving multiple steps (e.g., changing a tire or planting a flower) in which the steps are out of order; ask the client to sequence the steps in their correct order.

28. Assign the client a daily living task to carry out (e.g., shaving or dressing) while performing the steps in correct order; provide cues and redirection as needed ("What do you first?" "What happens next?") and fading cues as performance improves.

16. Provide reasonable solutions to everyday living problems. (29, 30, 31)

29. Present the client with hypo-thetical situations that require problem-solving skills and reasoned judgment (e.g., "What would you do if you were driv-ing and blew a tire?" "What would you do if you saw smoke coming out of the oven?"); guide the reasoning process and reinforce appropriate responses.

30. Present the client with open-ended problems (e.g., "What would you do if you wanted to go to the movies, and your children wanted to stay home and watch TV?") and have him/her provide alternative

solutions; reinforce reasonable responses.

31. Ask the client to demonstrate how he/she would solve an everyday problem from beginning to end (e.g., asking directions to the hospital vending room and then buying soda) using compensatory strategies (e.g., writing lists and taking notes to plan and carry out the task); reinforce prompt, efficient completion of the assignment.

17. Accurately interpret abstract material presented orally. (32, 33)

32. Read jokes, puns, and proverbial expressions to the client and ask him/her to interpret them; reinforce accurate interpretation.

33. Present the client with tasks that require him/her to determine cause-effect associations, draw reasonable conclusions, discern relationships (e.g., "What are some possible causes for house fires?"); score for the appropriateness of the responses.

18. Engage in speech at the conversational level using strategies that enhance staying on the topic. (34)

34. Instruct the client in the use of stereotyped expressions to use in conversation that will help him/her stay on topic and ensure that he/she understands what is said (e.g., "I understand" "Did you say . . . ?" "Is that clear?" "Do you understand what I'm saying?"); reinforce consistent use of the strategies.

19. Client and family consistently use a home carry-over program for communication. (35)

35. Develop a home carry-over program that includes the facilitative strategies and compensatory techniques most effective in maintaining the client's communication,

orientation, and memory skills; instruct the family/caregivers in the implementation of the program.

__. _____   __. _____
    _____   _____
__. _____   __. _____
    _____   _____
__. _____   __. _____
    _____   _____

DIAGNOSTIC SUGGESTIONS:

Axis I: 294.9   Cognitive Disorder NOS
                  307.9   Communication Disorder NOS
                  315.31   Expressive Language Disorder
                  315.32   Mixed Receptive-Expressive Language
                             Disorder

                  _____   _____
                  _____   _____

TRACHEOSTOMY AND VENTILATOR DEPENDENCE

BEHAVIORAL DEFINITIONS

1. An inability to achieve or maintain voicing because of tracheostomy tube placement resulting in a lack of oral communication.
2. Inability to maintain life-sustaining respiration without the assistance of mechanical ventilation.
3. Tracheostomy tube placement because of airway obstruction, poor secretion management, or poor airway protection.
4. Poor management of oral secretions.
5. Inability to maintain adequate nutrition via oral feeding alone.
6. Recurrent aspiration of food.
7. Reduced laryngeal strength and excursion.
8. Reduced oral-motor skills.

—. _____
   _____
—. _____
   _____
   _____
—. _____
   _____

LONG-TERM GOALS

1. Increase effective oral communication.
2. Effective use of an augmentative/alternative communication system in the absence of speech.
3. Adequate respiration without mechanical support.
4. Respiration for life sustenance using necessary mechanical support.

5. Effective management and care of tracheostomy and ventilation equipment.
6. Oral-motor and laryngeal skills adequate for the support of speech and oral feeding.
7. Oral intake to meet nutritional needs on the least restrictive diet.

—. _____

_____

—. _____

_____

_____

SHORT-TERM OBJECTIVES

THERAPEUTIC INTERVENTIONS

1. Cooperate with the medical assessment. (1)

1. Confer with the medical team (e.g., pulmonologist, respiratory therapist, and nurse) on the client's overall medical status and respiratory needs, including ventilation requirements, type of tracheostomy tube to be used, and secretion management.

2. Participate in the speech-language evaluation. (2)

2. Conduct a complete speech-language evaluation noting especially the client's ability to tolerate occlusion of the tracheostomy tube, breathe with the upper airway, phonate, and swallow; assess for the coexistence of other speech-language impairments (e.g., aphasia, dysarthria, or apraxia).

3. Family members and the client accept recommendations regarding respiratory management, communication, and swallowing status and agree on a treatment plan. (3)

3. In a multidisciplinary staffing, discuss with the family and caregivers the client's communicative and swallowing status and their implications for rehabilitation and prognosis; present an intervention plan for communication and swallowing.

4. Participate with family and caregivers in education regarding maintenance of mechanical ventilation and care of the tracheostomy site. (4)

4. With the respiratory therapist and nurse, instruct the client and caregivers (as far as is medically acceptable) in maintenance of the mechanical ventilation system and care of the tracheostomy site, including adjusting oxygen levels correctly, suctioning secretions, and maintaining hygiene of the tracheostomy site.

5. Stabilize breathing via the upper airway. (5, 6, 7)

5. Ask a nurse to suction the client and, according to established protocols, deflate the tracheostomy tube cuff, which will allow some exhaled air to bypass the inner cannula and enter the upper airway.

6. Ask the client to inhale and exhale slowly with the tracheostomy tube opening unoccluded, noting whether any air is passing through the nose and mouth; discontinue if he/she shows signs of anxiety or respiratory distress.

7. Manually occlude the tracheostomy tube opening, to increase the volume of air entering the upper airway, and ask the client to continue breathing; discontinue if the client shows signs of respiratory distress; reinflate the tracheostomy cuff and allow him/her to rest; attempt upper airway breathing at intervals until he/she demonstrates increased tolerance of the procedure.

6. Effectively manage upper airway secretions 90% of the time. (8, 9)

8. If the client tolerates breathing with the tracheostomy tube occluded for significant intervals, confer with the medical

team about initiating a program to systematically cap the tracheostomy tube, allowing him/her to breath via the upper airway exclusively for increased periods of time throughout the day.

9. After occluding the tracheostomy tube, ask the client to produce a sharp "cough-clear" to help expectorate airway secretions.

7. Carry out vocal fold adduction exercises with 90% accuracy. (10, 11)

10. Assist the client with a weak, nonproductive cough by placing both hands on his/her lower thoracic area and pushing firmly, to increase the volume of air to the vocal folds, as he/she coughs.

11. Ask the client to produce a sharp /ha-ha/, forcibly bringing the vocal folds together, as a prerequisite for voicing.

8. Achieve stable independent voicing. (12, 13)

12. Ask the client to inhale sharply and bring the vocal folds together in an effortful breath hold, ensuring glottal closure for protection of the airway during feeding.

13. When the client can breath using the upper airway without distress and can consistently adduct the vocal folds, ask him/her to phonate on /a/, noting the ability to sustain phonation, phonatory quality, and volume.

9. Achieve stable voicing and oral expression after modifying the tracheostomy tube. (14, 15)

14. Ask the client to phonate on other isolated vowels; as phonation stabilizes, introduce short words and phrases,

gradually proceeding to the sentence and conversational level.

15. For a client who cannot tolerate tracheostomy tube capping without respiratory distress, modify the type or size of the tracheostomy tube (e.g., introduce a tube with a fenestrated inner cannula), which will allow the client to inhale through the tube and redirect the air flow up to the level of the larynx to produce voicing.

10. Achieve stable voicing and oral expression using a one-way speaking valve. (16, 17, 18)

16. When tube alterations are made, ask the client to phonate; when phonation is stable, proceed to voiced production of words and phrases.

17. For the client who cannot tolerate capping, initiate the use of a one-way speaking valve (e.g., a Passy-Muir valve) to be placed on the tracheostomy tube, which will allow air to enter the tube and redirect the air flow up to the level of the larynx; on stabilization of voicing, proceed to production of words and phrases.

18. Confer with the medical team to schedule the client to wear the one-way speaking valve, gradually increasing the time that the valve is worn.

11. Communicate by mouthing words with 90% effectiveness if voicing cannot be achieved. (19, 20)

19. Review the basics of articulatory placement with the client, to increase his/her awareness of oral movements.

20. Teach the client to compensate for the lack of voicing by

overarticulating words; facilitate clarity of expression by encouraging him/her to use short words and phrases.

12. Effectively communicate using an electrolarynx if laryngeal voicing cannot be achieved. (21, 22, 23)

21. Demonstrate effective placement of a hand-held electrolarynx on the client's neck or under the chin.

22. Teach the client how to activate vibration of the electrolarynx while maintaining effective placement.

23. Teach the client to speak at a slow rate while overarticulating consonants, coordinating articulation with activation of the electrolarynx.

13. Communicate using an augmentative/alternative system. (24, 25, 26)

24. To meet the client's immediate care needs, instruct him/her and the care-givers in an alert system (e.g., using buzzers or call lights) to get staff's attention, and a yes-no system that will allow staff to question the client regarding his/her needs.

25. If the client has use of his/her hands, ask him/her to write messages on a note pad, point to letters on an alphabet board, or point to pictures.

26. If the client does not have use of his/her hands, assess him/her for an electronic communication system that uses printed or voice output; confer with occupational therapy and rehabilitation engineering to determine the most appropriate positioning of the client and the most efficient mode of access for the system.

14. Cooperate with a video-fluoroscopic swallow study. (27)

15. Increase the strength and mobility of the oral musculature using oral motor exercises with 90% effectiveness. (28, 29)

16. Increase glottal closure and laryngeal elevation to improve airway protection 95% of the time. (30, 31)

17. Carry out trial swallows until no aspiration is noted with light therapeutic feeding. (32, 33, 34)

27. Arrange a videofluoroscopic swallow evaluation to fully assess the client's swallowing function.

28. Instruct the client in lip strengthening exercises to facilitate lip closure and reduce spillage of food from the mouth by asking him/her to pucker-release his/her lips; ask the client to firmly close his/her lips on a tongue depressor for up to five seconds; perform each exercise in three sets of 10 repetitions each.

29. To improve the client's ability to orally manipulate a food bolus, instruct him/her in exercises to increase the strength and agility of tongue, including tongue protrusion-retraction, elevation-depression, and lateralization; ask the client to perform each exercise in three sets of 10 repetitions each.

30. Ask the client to produce a high-pitched /i/ sound and hold it for three to five seconds; practice in three sets of five repetitions.

31. Ask the client to swallow hard to elevate the larynx and close the glottis; repeat up to 10 times.

32. Before feeding, ask nursing to deflate the tracheostomy tube cuff, which will permit air to pass up to the larynx, allowing the client to cough and expectorate secretions, as well as helping the SLP to detect aspiration.

33. Cap or manually occlude the tracheostomy tube and present the client with a small amount of puree, observing his/her manipulation and transit of the bolus, swallow reflex initiation, and laryngeal elevation; note any signs of aspiration (i.e., coughing or gurgly vocal quality).

34. Rule out gross aspiration by presenting the client with a small amount of puree mixed with blue food coloring; ask nursing to suction the client's tracheostomy tube at 15-minute intervals over a two-hour period after trial feeding, noting whether any blue coloring is present in the suctioned material (Blue Dye Test); lack of blue color in the suctioned material indicates a negative result.

18. Demonstrate tolerance of therapeutic oral feeding with gradually increased texture of food. (35, 36)

35. Gradually increase the texture of the client's food by mixing soft chunks with the puree; monitor his/her tolerance of the mixture.

36. When the client demonstrates tolerance of the puree/chunky mixture, eliminate the puree and introduce soft foods; gradually increase the amounts fed to the client.

19. Demonstrate tolerance of the least restrictive oral diet. (37)

37. Confer with the dietitian on the most appropriate oral diet for the client; also confer with the physician and nursing staff on systematically transitioning him/her to full oral intake by gradually reducing enteral feeding and increasing oral feeding.

20. Tolerate the decannulation process and removal of the tracheostomy tube. (38)

38. Assist in the medical team's decision-making process regarding the client's status for weaning from artificial ventilation, addressing such issues as alertness, nutritional status, and medical stability. (*Note:* The pulmonologist, respiratory therapist, and nurse must make the primary decision to wean.)

__. _____   __. _____

    _____   _____

__. _____   __. _____

    _____   _____

__. _____   __. _____

    _____   _____

DIAGNOSTIC SUGGESTIONS:

Axis I: 799.9   Diagnosis Deferred
            V71.09   No Diagnosis or Condition

            _____   _____

            _____   _____

TRAUMATIC BRAIN INJURY—ADULT

BEHAVIORAL DEFINITIONS

1. Documented injury to the brain.
2. Difficulty maintaining awareness and/or attention.
3. Difficulty with executive functions for organized and goal-directed behavior.
4. Presence of anomia.
5. Lack of speech clarity related to respiratory, articulation, and/or resonance deficits.
6. Auditory and reading comprehension deficits (i.e., receptive aphasia).
7. Verbal and written expression deficits (i.e., expressive aphasia).
8. Difficulty with swallowing.
9. Impulsivity and poor judgment in social situations.

__. _____
   _____

__. _____
   _____

__. _____
   _____

LONG-TERM GOALS

1. Become aware of and learn to attend to sensory stimuli.
2. Develop strategies for coping with long- and short-term memory deficits.
3. Develop clear and intelligible speech in conversations.
4. Improve word retrieval in conversations.
5. Engage in meaningful, connected conversations.

6. Develop strategies for organizing and using information to solve every-day problems.
7. Develop realistic insight into one's own strengths and weaknesses.
8. Family and caregivers structure the living environment in a way that maintains the client's orientation and memory skills.
9. Family and caregivers establish realistic expectations for the client's cognitive-communicative skills and work collaboratively with the speech-language pathologist (SLP) and other professionals to develop effective treatment strategies.

__. _____
   _____

__. _____
   _____

__. _____
   _____

SHORT-TERM OBJECTIVES

1. Cooperate with a medical/neurological evaluation. (1)

2. Participate willingly in a cognitive-communicative evaluation to determine daily communicative functioning in different contexts. (2, 3)

THERAPEUTIC INTERVENTIONS

1. Confer with the medical team on the client's current diagnosis, medical history, previous treatment, and rehabilitative potential.

2. Administer a speech-language evaluation, focusing on the deficit areas relevant to traumatic brain injury (e.g., attention, orientation, memory, verbal skills, executive decisions, and problem-solving skills).

3. Document the client's communicative skills periodically as he/she improves by using informal assessment procedures, such as observing his/her communicative needs in various situations and conducting collaborative hypothesis testing during daily activities with the

client and his/her family and caregivers to determine his/her present cognitive-communicative strengths and weaknesses.

3. Cooperate with a complete oral-motor examination. (4)

4. Evaluate the client's oral-motor functioning by first observing the visible structure of his/her face, lips, teeth, tongue, and hard and soft palate and then assess how he/she uses specific structures important for speech and language production (e.g., movement, strength, and closure of the lips; strength, protrusion, retraction, and lateralization of the tongue; or movement of the soft palate when producing the /a/ phoneme).

4. Participate willingly in an audiological assessment. (5, 6)

5. Conduct a pure-tone audiological screening of the client at 500, 1000, 2000, and 4000 Hz at 20 dB.

6. Refer the client to an audiologist for a complete evaluation if results of the audiological screening indicate a need for further assessment.

5. Family members and the client provide information relevant to a speech-language evaluation. (7)

7. Solicit information from family members, and, if appropriate, from the client regarding the client's level of education, occupation, and overall communicative sophistication to design a treatment plan consistent with his/her communicative needs.

6. Family, caregivers, and the client, if appropriate, accept the recommendations developed, and collaboratively select communicative behav-

8. Conduct regular meetings with the client's family, caregivers, and other relevant professionals to develop and modify collaborative intervention

ioral goals that adhere to the client's priorities and cultural values. (8, 9)

7. Maintain attention to task 90% of the time. (10, 11, 12)

8. Accurately identify significant others with 95% accuracy. (13, 14)

strategies as the client makes progress.

9. Select specific communicative situations as targets for intervention for the client based on his/her cognitive, linguistic, occupational, and social communicative needs.

10. Teach the client to focus his/her attention by placing stimulus material in his/her visual field and manually move his/her head while giving the verbal cue, "Look" until his/her gaze meets the materials; gradually fade the physical prompt until the client can maintain his/her gaze on the task when given verbal or gestural cues only.

11. Help the client maintain his/her attention for longer periods by setting a timer to ring at specified intervals during a task and instructing the client to maintain attention during the timed intervals; redirect him/her to the stimulus materials if he/she shows signs of wandering.

12. Teach the client self-control strategies for staying on task (e.g., rehearsing self-directed questions) that redirect his/her attention (e.g., "What am I doing?" "Am I drifting?" "What should I be doing?").

13. Obtain photographs of the client's family and significant others, including hospital staff; label the photographs with each person's name and his/her relationship to the client; place these in a categorized notebook

(e.g., "Family," "Friends," "Staff") and refer to the photographs when speaking to him/her about people.

14. Ask the client to address people by name when they are encountered throughout the day; cue the client to facilitate identification (e.g., "Here's your nurse. What's her name?").

9. Provide accurate information on time, date, and simple schedule of activities. (15, 16, 17, 18)

15. To increase the client's accuracy in perception of time, encourage the spontaneous use of a clock and wristwatch by ensuring that he/she has a clock with large numbers in his/her room and a wristwatch to wear; during the session, ask him/her to take note of the time and reinforce his/her accurate time perception.

16. Provide the client with a wall calendar for his her room and a pocket calendar to carry; each day, have him/her cross out the previous day's date on the calendar and direct him/her to the present date ("Yesterday was Wednesday the 10th. Today is Thursday the 11th."). Teach the client to refer to the calendar at intervals to remind him/herself of the day.

17. To help the client maintain an accurate perception of the day of the week, select significant events that occur consistently during the week for him/her to use as markers for reckoning days (e.g., "Yesterday we had Bingo. Bingo is on Tuesday. So today must be Wednesday.").

18. Establish a schedule of daily activities with the client, including stipulation of the time, location, and people involved; rehearse the schedule with the client, cueing as necessary, and gradually fading the number of cues until he/she can use the schedule spontaneously or with minimal cues.

10. Consistently use compensatory strategies to aid memory. (19)

19. Instruct the client in compensatory, short-term memory strategies (e.g., making "to do" lists, keeping files of important names, posting reminders in prominent places, and arranging the living environment in a consistent recognizable way).

11. Accurately navigate around the living environment, including identifying and locating his/her own room. (20, 21)

20. Familiarize the client with the living environment by taking him/her on repeated walking tours of the various wings where he/she will be spending time, noting important landmarks along the way (e.g., the nurses station, TV lounge, the dining room) to enhance memory.

21. Provide the client with a floor plan of the living environment in a pocket notebook; as the client's familiarity with the living environment increases, ask him/her to show the way to a particular area or department using the previously learned landmarks and floor plan as cues to lead him/her to the desired area.

12. Carry out directives of increasing complexity in everyday activities with 90% accuracy. (22, 23)

22. Ask the client to carry out functional directives, providing modeling and verbal direction appropriate to the level at which

the client is able to process the information; start with one-step directives and gradually move to two-step directives as the client's success increases to 90%.

23. Increase the number of steps in the directives the client is to carry out, gradually fading the modeling until he/she is able to carry out multistep directives given only oral input; provide encouragement and reinforcement of effort and success.

13. Sequence events of daily living in correct chronological order. (24, 25)

24. Give the client written tasks that present an activity involving multiple steps (e.g., planting a garden or scrambling eggs) in which the steps are out of order; ask him/her to sequence the steps correctly.

25. Assign the client a task of daily living (e.g., shaving or preparing a snack) performing the steps in correct order; provide cues and redirection as needed ("What do you do first?" "What happens next?"); fade the cues as performance improves.

14. Demonstrate improved word-finding skills to a 90% accuracy level. (26, 27)

26. Assist the client in improving his/her word-finding skills through the administration of responsive naming tasks, presenting him/her with a picture and an open-ended sentence ("You write with a ____?"); ask for a one-word answer.

27. Perform confrontative naming tasks, presenting the client with a picture and asking, "What's this?"; provide a description of the picture or a first phoneme cue if needed.

15. Demonstrate improved verbal categorization skills to a 90% accuracy level. (28, 29)

28. Give the client a broad verbal category (e.g., animals) and ask him/her to name as many examples as possible.

29. Give the client the constituent elements of a verbal category and ask him/her to give the name of the category that comprises the elements (e.g., "Leaves, branches, and bark belong to what?" "A tree.").

16. Reduce extraneous, non-relevant verbalizations to 10%. (30, 31)

30. Agree with the client on the use of a hand signal that the SLP will use to indicate that he/she is rambling inappropriately (e.g., holding the hand up to indicate stop); when the SLP gestures stop, the client stops talking and awaits redirection.

31. Increase the client's awareness of his/her lack of focus to his/her conversation by allowing him/her to listen to a tape-recorded sample of his/her spontaneous speech; assist the client in noting the digressions from the main topic.

17. Demonstrate appropriate conversational turn-taking 90% of the time. (32, 33)

32. Practice asking and answering questions using board games; reinforce the client's successful turn-taking in conversation and redirect him/her for failure to adhere to turn-taking.

33. Conduct mock interviews in which the client asks the SLP about work, hobbies, and family; switch roles; guide him/her in the use of appropriate conversational exchange.

18. Engage in conversation, using strategies that enhance topic maintenance. (34)

34. Teach the client to use stereotype expressions during conversation to help him/her stay on

19. Demonstrate accurate self-awareness by identifying his/her own problematic communication concerns. (35, 36, 37)

topic (e.g., "Do you understand what I'm saying?" "Did you say . . . ?" "Is that clear?").

35. Arrange for the client to meet with or view videotapes of other clients with traumatic brain injury; discuss the problematic behaviors of the other clients, directing his/her attention to the target behaviors until he/she is able to identify them accurately.

36. Ask the client to view a videotape of himself/herself, directing him/her to note any similarities between his/her problematic behavior and that observed in the videotape of other clients; on repeated viewings of the tape, direct the client's attention to problematic behaviors and communication strengths.

37. Ask the client to write a list of his/her communication strengths and weaknesses; discuss with him/her the accuracy of the list as an indicator of his/her self-awareness.

20. Provide reasonable solutions to problems of everyday living. (38, 39)

38. Role-play problematic daily living situations, directing the client though the problem-solving process of gathering and organizing relevant information, identifying and weighing options, and developing and implementing a plan.

39. Ask the client to demonstrate how he/she would solve an everyday problem from beginning to end (e.g., washing the dishes); write a list of the steps necessary to carry out the task (e.g., moving dirty dishes from

the table to the sink, rinsing the dishes, placing them in dishwasher [or washing them by hand], placing dried and clean dishes in the cabinet); reinforce prompt, efficient completion of the assignment.

21. Orally summarize a written passage, identifying the central theme and important secondary information. (40, 41)

40. Teach the client to identify the main and secondary ideas after reading a passage out loud to the SLP; ask him/her highlight or outline the information.

41. After the client reads the passage to himself/herself, ask him/her to orally paraphrase the pertinent information from it, using the highlighted information as an organizational guide.

22. Recount recent events, accurately noting salient information. (42, 43, 44)

42. To help the client recount meetings and outings, instruct him/her in the use of a flowsheet to record the nature of the outing, persons involved, and chronology of events; accompany the client on outings, illustrating the use of the flowsheet until he/she can use it independently.

43. Ask the client to orally recount a recent outing (e.g., a trip to the mall or a visit home) using the flowsheet as an organizational guide; reinforce success and redirect for failure.

44. Using material recorded on the flowsheet, teach the client to identify the main idea of the outing and secondary ideas; ask him/her to write a narrative of up to five sentences, critiquing the writing for organization and appropriate subordination of ideas.

23. Client and family consistently use a home carry-over program for communication. (45)

24. Client uses two to three strategies appropriate for managing dysphagia. (46)

45. Develop a home carry-over program that includes the facilitative and compensatory strategies most effective in maintaining the client's communication, orientation, and memory skills; instruct the family and caregivers in the implementation of the program.

46. Teach the client and caregivers, if appropriate, strategies for dysphagia intervention (see Dysphagia—Adult chapter in this *Planner*).

—. _____

—. _____

—. _____

—. _____

—. _____

—. _____

DIAGNOSTIC SUGGESTIONS:

Axis I: 294.9   Cognitive Disorder NOS
307.9   Communication Disorder NOS
315.32   Mixed Receptive-Expressive Language Disorder

_____   _____

_____   _____

TRAUMATIC BRAIN INJURY— PEDIATRIC

BEHAVIORAL DEFINITIONS

1. Documented injury to the brain.
2. Inability to maintain awareness and/or attention.
3. Difficulty with executive functions for organized and goal-directed behavior.
4. Presence of anomia.
5. Lack of speech clarity related to respiratory, articulation, and/or resonance deficits.
6. Auditory and reading comprehension deficits (i.e., receptive aphasia).
7. Verbal and written expression deficits (i.e., expressive aphasia).
8. Difficulty with swallowing.
9. Social interaction deficits with peers.

___. _____

_____

___. _____

_____

___. _____

_____

LONG-TERM GOALS

1. Become aware of and learn to attend to sensory stimuli.
2. Develop strategies for coping with long- and short-term memory deficits.
3. Develop clear and intelligible speech in conversations.
4. Improve word retrieval in conversation.

5. Develop strategies for organizing and using information to solve everyday problems.
6. Develop social interaction skills appropriate for age, dialect, and cultural expectations in various communicative contexts and monitor success.
7. Develop realistic insight into one's own strengths and weaknesses.
8. Parents structure the living environment in a way that maintains the client's orientation and memory skills.
9. Parents establish realistic expectations for their child's cognitive-communicative skills, and work collaboratively with the speech-language pathologist (SLP) and other professionals to develop effective treatment strategies.

—. _____

_____

—. _____

_____

—. _____

_____

SHORT-TERM OBJECTIVES

THERAPEUTIC INTERVENTIONS

1. Cooperate with a medical/ neurological evaluation. (1)

1. Confer with the medical team on the client's current diagnosis, medical history, previous treatment, and rehabilitative potential.

2. Participate willingly in cognitive-communicative evaluation to determine daily communicative functioning in different contexts. (2, 3)

2. Document the client's communicative skills by using standardized assessments (e.g., see Scales for Cognitive Ability for Traumatic Brain Injury by Adamovich and Henderson or the Pediatric Test of Brain Injury by Hotz, Helm-Estabrooks, and Nelson).

3. Document the client's communicative skills periodically as he/ she improves by using informal assessment procedures, such as

3. Cooperate with a complete oral-motor examination. (4)

4. Participate willingly in an audiological assessment. (5, 6)

5. Parents and other professionals contribute to the interpretation of evaluation information. (7, 8)

observing his/her communicative needs in various situations and conducting collaborative hypothesis testing during daily activities with the client and his/her family and the hospital or school staff to determine his/her present cognitive-communicative strengths and weaknesses.

4. Evaluate the client's oral-motor functioning by first observing the visible structure of his/her face, lips, teeth, tongue, and hard and soft palate and then assess how he/she uses specific structures important for speech and language production (e.g., movement, strength, and closure of the lips; strength, protrusion, retraction, and lateralization of the tongue; or movement of the soft palate when producing the /a/ phoneme).

5. Conduct a pure-tone audiological screening of the client at 500, 1000, 2000, and 4000 Hz at 20 dB.

6. Refer the client to an audiologist for a complete evaluation, if results of the audiological screening indicate a need for further assessment.

7. Ask the parents and other professionals to contribute information on the client's previous developmental milestones and educational status, current medical status, other professional interventions, communicative attempts in different settings, and social and family concerns.

8. Parents seek ongoing trans-disciplinary evaluations for the client from an educational psychologist, teacher, pediatric neurologist, physical therapist, social worker, occupational therapist, audiologist, and other relevant professionals to document the cognitive, educational, health, hearing, daily living, and motor skills important for developing appropriate communicative interventions.

6. Parents and, if appropriate, the client accept the recommendations developed and collaboratively select communicative behavioral goals that adhere to the family's priorities and cultural values. (9, 10)

9. Conduct regular meetings with the client's parents and other relevant professionals to develop and modify collaborative intervention strategies as the client makes progress.

10. Select specific communicative situations as targets for intervention for the client based on his/her cognitive, linguistic, social, and academic communicative needs.

7. Parents and teachers verbalize realistic expectations for the client and utilize positive and supportive resources. (11, 12)

11. Explain to the client's parents, teachers, and other relevant professionals the relationships between his/her behaviors related to his/her traumatic brain injury and his/her communication skills.

12. Provide helpful references and resources on traumatic brain injury for the client's parents and teachers.

8. Parents and, if appropriate, school or hospital staff, implement appropriate environmental supports, strategies, and behavioral

13. Explore with the client's parents and teachers what environmental supports are needed to maximize his/her communicative success (e.g., posting daily schedules at

consequences that enhance the client's cognitive-communicative success. (13)

9. Attend to sensory stimuli for increasing lengths of time as appropriate for the phase of improvement and type and location of brain injury. (14, 15, 16)

home and at school, providing written rules for participating in games or learning centers, providing graphic organizers, and/or removing overwhelming sensory materials).

14. If the client is unable to respond or only able to respond with generalized responses (e.g., at Levels I or II on the Rancho Scale of Cognition and Language), teach the parents and staff to use short, simple phrases and speak about the client's interests (e.g., family members or friends or quietly explain medical procedures such as changing feeding tubes or bedding, or maintaining hygiene).

15. If the client is able to provide generalized or localized responses (e.g., at Levels II or III on the Rancho Scale of Cognition and Language), teach the parents to help the client with oral-motor exercises (e.g., gently massaging his/her facial muscles, moving his/her facial muscles in different positions, or providing oral stimulation for him/her using a soft Nuk brush).

16. If the client is at Level IV or V on the Rancho Scale of Cognition and Language, teach the parents to help client orient to time, people, and place in his/her immediate environment by asking the client questions and gently correcting inappropriate statements and providing visual supports using pictures, schedules, and clocks.

10. Complete one task and move to another task successfully four out of five times. (17, 18)

11. If nonverbal, communicate during daily routines by using augmentative/ alternative communication systems with 80% accuracy. (19)

12. Use clear and intelligible speech in conversations with others. (20)

13. Parents and/or client use two to three strategies appropri- ate for managing the client's dysphagia. (21)

14. Follow increasingly more complex oral and/or written directions with 80% accuracy. (22, 23)

17. Make written and/or graphic checklists for the client that outline the steps for common daily activities and/or assignments; teach him/her, first, to systematically check off the steps as he/she completes them and then to make his/her own checklists for completing daily tasks.

18. Reinforce the client for inde- pendently recognizing and then communicating successfully task completion.

19. Use augmentative/alternative communication with the client to interact in everyday situations (see the Augmentative/ Alternative Communication chapter in this *Planner*).

20. Use strategies with the client for developing intelligible speech for daily activities (see the Dysarthria chapter in this *Planner*).

21. Teach the client and parents, if appropriate, strategies for dys- phagia intervention (see the Dysphagia—Child chapter in this *Planner*).

22. Limit oral directions for the client to one directive while using simple gestures and facial expressions to enhance the verbal information during routine activities, such as hygiene, play, classroom, or household chore routines, and then provide adequate time for him/her to indicate that he/she correctly comprehended the direction; reinforce compliance.

23. Teach the client to ask his/her teachers, parents, and others to slow down and repeat the oral directions one at a time so that he/she can remember what to do.

15. Sequence the events of real-life situations into correct chronological order. (24, 25)

24. Add visual cues (e.g., written directions or symbolic pictures) for routine events by making story boards or communication books that picture each explicit step in common tasks (e.g., handing out snacks in a preschool room, completing assignments, putting personal items in his/her locker, or setting the dinner table); ask the client to follow the event's sequences as he/she is completing the task; reinforcing his/her successful achievement.

25. Model the steps of a routine event for the client before asking him/her to complete the event sequence; for each task, ask him/her to imitate your words and actions and then add more complex sequential tasks over time as he/she increases his/her ability to attend for longer periods of time.

16. Use two to three different strategies for improving word retrieval. (26, 27, 28)

26. Teach the client to describe the main features of objects or pictures (e.g., color, size, shape, function, or other identifying features).

27. Using a barrier, teach the client to gesture or draw an object he/she sees so that an uninformed person can easily identify the object without seeing it.

28. Model the use of carrier phrases (e.g., "You brush your teeth with a ____") to elicit specific words from the client; encourage significant others to use carrier phrases to prompt the client.

17. Implement three strategies for learning age-appropriate academic material. (29, 30, 31)

29. Explore memory strategies for learning academic information with the client, such as using verbal mediation (e.g., saying the steps of the task out loud), visualization techniques (using pictures or symbols that represent the information), or chunking similar types of information (e.g., putting similar tasks together into superordinate categories).

30. Teach the client to consolidate new information by rewriting notes using graphic organizers (e.g., word webs and charts).

31. Teach the client to use note-taking strategies, such as paying attention to the teacher's cues (e.g., listening to changes in pitch, watching special gestures, or writing key words on the board), using two columns, one for the teacher's information and one for questions and notes to oneself to organize the information, using an audio tape recorder, or having a peer provide notes.

18. Tell a story with at least three events in logical sequence, as developmentally appropriate. (32, 33, 34)

32. Teach the client to use a scripted story grammar recipe (e.g., setting the scene, describing the characters, sequencing the events, describing the conflict, and stating the resolution) to tell stories with a coherent beginning, middle and end (see

the *Story Grammar Marker Kit* by Moreau and Fidrych-Puzzo).

33. Help the client tell a story by using three to five sequential photographs of an event in his/her life (e.g., a birthday party, a pet's antics, or a recent trip to the doctor).

34. After reading a short story, ask the client to retell, draw, or gesture the main events in the correct sequence.

19. Summarize information found in a written paragraph with 90% accuracy. (35, 36)

35. Teach the client to use a variety of graphic organizers (e.g., word webs, timelines, or organizational charts) to illustrate the main ideas in paragraphs from his/her academic textbooks(see *Kidspiration* computer software at http://www.engagingminds.com).

36. Teach the client how to identify main and subordinate ideas by highlighting or underlining in his/her academic textbooks; ask him/her to summarize these key ideas.

20. Write an organized para-graph using correct syntax with at least three substan-tiated details, as appropriate for age. (37, 38)

37. Teach the client to choose a topic and brainstorm three main ideas with two to three details of that topic then teach him/her to write three sentences using those ideas; teach him/her to write an introductory sentence and a similar conclusion sentence.

38. Provide an introductory and conclusion sentence from the client's academic work and then help him/her write three descrip-tive sentences with sufficient detail to make a complete

21. Take more than three conversational turns on the same topic with appropriate verbal and nonverbal communication. (39, 40)

22. Engage in social interactions appropriately in various situations with different conversational partners. (41, 42, 43)

23. Understand developmentally appropriate abstract language with 80% accuracy. (44, 45)

paragraph, using the knowledge he/she learned in class.

39. First, teach the client to recognize an abrupt change in a conversational topic by someone and then teach him/her to take at least three conversational turns on the same topic before moving on to another topic.

40. Teach the client to identify changes in a speaker's eye gaze and use of pauses that allow him/her to take turns at the appropriate conversational moment.

41. Use peers to coach and model age-appropriate social communication for the client.

42. Help the client to determine specific situations (e.g., having to complete an undesirable or difficult task) that trigger inappropriate communicative behaviors and then use modeling and behavioral rehearsal to teach alternative positive communica-tive behaviors in response to the identified troublesome situations.

43. Instruct the client's parents or teachers to video record him/her interacting with family members or peers; review the video with the client to identify his/her appropriate and inappropriate social interaction and the ante-cedent events that preceded the inappropriate communicative behaviors.

44. Use age-appropriate books to teach figurative language (e.g., *Quick as a Cricket* by Wood, *A Collection of Similes and*

Metaphors by Body, or *Shall I Compare Thee: A Witty Collection of Quotable Similes* by Jarski); make flashcards for practicing the literal and figurative meanings found in the books.

45. Ask the client to make an expandable dictionary of figurative language to use as a reference for his/her academic work; have him/her include drawings/definitions that contrast literal and figurative definitions.

__. _____   __. _____

_____   _____

__. _____   __. _____

_____   _____

__. _____   __. _____

_____   _____

DIAGNOSTIC SUGGESTIONS:

Axis I:	307.9	Communication Disorder NOS
	315.32	Mixed Receptive-Expressive Language Disorder
	_____	_____
	_____	_____

VOICE DISORDERS

BEHAVIORAL DEFINITIONS

1. The voice has a breathy, half-whispered quality because of excessive escape of air from the glottis.
2. The voice has a harsh, strained, rough quality because of irregular phonation, unacceptably low pitch, and excessive pharyngeal tension.
3. The voice has a strident, piercing, metallic quality because of irregular phonation, unacceptably high pitch, and excessive pharyngeal tension.
4. The voice has a hypernasal, whining quality, with inappropriate nasalization of vowels and weak production of plosives and fricatives.
5. The voice has a hyponasal, stuffy quality, like having a cold.
6. The voice has a throaty, booming, cavernous quality with unacceptably low habitual pitch and excessive pharyngeal tension.
7. The voice has a thin, shallow, weak quality, often inappropriate for the speaker's age or gender.
8. Speech lacks emotional interest and variety with prosodic features that are monotonous or stereotypic.
9. The habitual pitch level for speaking is unacceptably high or low.
10. The voice is judged by listeners as interfering with effective communication in everyday settings.
11. The voice is perceived by the speaker as a social or vocational impairment.

—. _____

_____

—. _____

_____

—. _____

_____

LONG-TERM GOALS

1. Demonstrate understanding of the vocal elements of phonation, pitch, resonance, and prosody.
2. Engage in speech at the conversational level using functional phonation, acceptable habitual pitch, balanced resonance, and appropriate prosody.
3. Maintain a program of good vocal hygiene by developing an awareness of behaviors and lifestyle conditions that may be hazardous to the voice.
4. Develop proprioceptive and auditory self-monitoring skills for discriminating functional from ineffective vocal behaviors.

—. _____
_____

—. _____
_____

—. _____
_____

SHORT-TERM OBJECTIVES

1. Cooperate with a medical examination of the larynx (direct or indirect laryngo-scopy) to rule out an organic basis for the voice disorder. (1, 2)

2. Client or parents provide the SLP with any additional medical history that may be relevant to the health and use of the voice. (3)

THERAPEUTIC INTERVENTIONS

1. Assist the client in obtaining the necessary referral to an otolaryngologist.

2. Confer with the otolaryngologist regarding whether the voice disorder has an organic basis that requires medical management or whether it is functional and amenable to behavioral intervention; convey this information to the client.

3. Obtain any additional medical information that may have relevance to the client's daily vocal use, including frequent upper respiratory infections, tonsil or adenoid problems, or excessive smoking or drinking.

3. Client or parents provide lifestyle information on customary vocal hygiene and the typical manner in which the voice is used in natural settings and situations. (4)

4. Participate in the voice evaluation. (5)

5. Accept the SLP's diagnosis of the voice disorder and recommendations in selecting the vocal behaviors to modify. (6)

6. Establish a baseline of inappropriate vocal use by charting the frequency of vocally abusive behaviors as they occur throughout the day in natural settings. (7, 8)

4. Obtain a history of the client's daily vocal use at work (does the client have a job that makes excessive demands on the voice, such as coaching, teaching aerobics, or talking over loud machinery?), at school (does the client talk loudly on the play-ground or in the lunchroom?), and at home (is there frequent shouting or loud talking over background noise?).

5. Administer the voice evaluation, analyzing phonation, pitch, resonance and prosody, and the interaction of these components, obtaining a baseline level of functioning by tape recording the client reading and speaking spontaneously; identify the behaviors causing the disorder and determine whether the disordered areas are amenable to intervention by experimenting with various facilitative techniques.

6. Give feedback to the client on the results of the voice evaluation; select the vocal behaviors to be modified and discuss the overall treatment program with the client or parents.

7. Assist the client in identifying his/her vocally abusive behaviors (e.g., excessive shouting, talking with excessive pharyngeal tension, loud talking on the playground, talking over loud background noise, and frequent throat clearing).

8. Instruct the client in a method of recording the frequency of

7. Increase phonatory function for improved voicing by reducing laryngeal hypertension with 90% accuracy. (9, 10, 11)

8. Increase phonatory function for improved voicing by increasing laryngeal tension with 90% accuracy. (12, 13)

vocally abusive behaviors throughout the day by using a small note pad.

9. Instruct the client in a variety of relaxation exercises (e.g., rotating the head while gently phonating "ah"; have him/her contrast tension versus relaxation by deliberately tightening the neck and shoulder muscles and then releasing).

10. Teach the client how to reduce laryngeal hypertension by modeling a "yawn-sigh" using a full, open throat and gentle release of air while phonating "ah"; have the client repeat and stabilize a relaxed "yawn-sigh."

11. If the client is a child, teach the concepts "rough voice" and "smooth voice," modeling each for contrastive purposes and having the child imitate; stabilize the use of smooth voice by having the child make up phrases and sentences or describe pictures while playing turn-taking games.

12. Increase the client's vocal fold adduction to reduce air leakage from the glottis by having the client place his/her hands against a table and vigorously push away while sharply phonating "ah"; repeat several times.

13. Instruct the client in correct abdominal-diaphragmatic breathing techniques; contrasting this with shallow clavicular breathing; when he/she can consistently imitate

9. Use functional phonation in speech from the word to conversational level. (14, 15, 16)

abdominal-diaphragmatic breathing, incorporate its use in speaking phrases and sentences.

14. Shape the "ah" of the "yawn-sigh" into other vowels (e.g., "oo," "aw," "oh") using the vowels as initial sounds in syllables and words; gradually fade the exaggerated features of the yawn-sigh and increase the length of utterance to the phrase and sentence levels.

15. Have the client read passages containing large numbers of lax vowels such as "ih," "eh," and "a" to facilitate reducing laryngeal hypertension.

16. Teach the client how to improve laryngeal hypofunction by asking him/her to count or say the alphabet while placing his/her hands against a table and vigorously pushing away and sharply phonating "ah"; repeat several times; incorporate short phrases while pushing; fade the pushing while maintaining the sharpness of the glottal attack when speaking.

10. Locate the optimal pitch level for speech with 90% accuracy. (17, 18, 19)

17. Using a piano or pitch pipe, find the lowest tone the client can hum without excessive glottal fry; have the client hum up the musical scale two-and-a-half steps (the interval of a fourth) and then raise or lower the pitch by half steps to find the pitch the client can hum most comfortably (that will be the optimal pitch).

18. For clients unable to match tones to a piano or pitch pipe,

have him/her say "mm-hmm"; the second syllable will be the client's optimal pitch; have the client locate his/her optimal pitch on request.

19. If the client is a child, instruct him/her in the concepts of "high voice," "low voice," and voice that is "just right," modeling each and having the child imitate; stabilize the use of "just right" voice by having the child make up phrases and sentences or describe pictures in "just right" voice while playing turn-taking games.

11. Extend the use of optimal pitch in speech from a single word to conversational level with 90% accuracy at each level. (20)

20. Stabilize the client's use of optimal pitch by having him/her hum it on /m/ or /n/; use these as initial sounds in syllables and words (e.g., "mm" is extended to "mah" then "mine"); increase the length of utterances from the word to the sentence level.

12. Demonstrate an under-standing of the dynamic interactions of the oral, nasal, and pharyngeal cavities and their acoustic characteristics in producing vocal resonance. (21)

21. Instruct the client in the struc-ture and interactions of the nasal, oral, and pharyngeal cavi-ties, of how they may be altered in size and shape during speech to produce the differing vocal resonances (i.e., model the vari-ous types of vocal resonance: nasal, denasal, throaty, and thin), having him/her correctly iden-tify the differing resonances when modeled to him/her in contrastive pairs (e.g., nasal ver-sus denasal, thin versus throaty).

13. Reduce hypernasal quality caused by excessive nasal resonance by increasing oral resonance. (22, 23)

22. Instruct the client to increase vo-cal intensity and mouth opening during speech to increase oral resonance and indirectly reduce nasal resonance.

23. Instruct the client in the kinesthetic aspects of velar movement by asking him/her to use a mirror to visually inspect the movement of the velum when producing nasal and nonnasal sounds; have the client impound air in the oral cavity by blowing up his/her cheeks and holding to get the feel of the velum against the rear wall of the pharynx and then produce minimal pairs (e.g., "pie-my," "pa-ma") to get the feel of velar movement, as well as contrast nonnasal versus nasal sounds.

14. Reduce excessive pharyngeal resonance causing throaty vocal quality by increasing oral resonance. (24, 25)

24. Decrease the size of the client's laryngopharynx and improve the balance of the oral and pharyngeal cavities by instructing him/her in frontal positioning of the tongue in the oral cavity; direct his/her tongue tip behind the upper front teeth, facilitating frontal tongue placement by having him/her read lists words containing lingua-alveolar phonemes (e.g., "tea" or "knee")

25. Directly reduce the size of the client's laryngopharynx by digitally pushing the thyroid cartilage up; have him/her phonate while holding the thyroid cartilage and note the difference in vocal quality.

15. Reduce thin vocal quality by increasing oral and pharyngeal resonance with 90% accuracy. (26, 27)

26. Instruct the client in posterior positioning of the tongue to increase the dimensions of the oral cavity; stabilize rear positioning of the tongue by practicing low back vowels ("oo," "aw," "oh") and words

containing these vowels in initial positions.

27. Directly increase the size of the client's laryngopharynx by pushing the thyroid cartilage down; have him/her phonate while holding the thyroid cartilage and note the difference in vocal quality.

16. Extend the use of balanced vocal resonance from the word to the conversational level. (28, 29, 30)

28. Teach the client to reduce hypernasality by having him/her read passages of words in which no nasal phonemes are present; have him/her judge his/her production by marking each syllable in which he/she hears nasality (see in Chapter 3 *Improving Voice and Articulation* by Fisher, and Chapter 10 *Modifying Vocal Behavior* by Moncur and Brackett).

29. Tape record the client reading passages loaded with front vowels and tongue-tip sounds to improve the resonant balance of the oral and pharyngeal cavities; ask him/her to listen to the recording and mark words that sound unusually throaty, increasing the length of the reading passages as allowed.

30. Tape record the client reading passages filled with back vowels; ask him/her to mark words that sound unusually thin while increasing the length of the reading passages.

17. Increase the emotional interest and expression of speech by varied use of the

31. Teach the client how the prosodic features of pitch variation, intensity, and rate can

prosodic features of pitch variation, rate, and intensity. (31, 32, 33, 34)

increase the expressiveness and emotional interest of what is spoken.

32. Ask the client to mark words to be emphasized in a reading passage and then use modeling and behavior rehearsal to teach him/her the use of greater vocal intensity for increased emphasis in speaking; critique the client for effectiveness of expression.

33. Count the number of words the client reads in one minute; if the rate is above 180 or below 150 words per minute (wpm), have him/her adjust his/her rate by using a stopwatch when reading and bringing his/her rate within the 150 to 180 wpm range.

34. Ask the client to mark and label a reading passage with varying intonation patterns and then use modeling and behavior rehearsal to teach him/her various intonation patterns (e.g., declarative statements, question forms, embedded phrases); critique the client for effectiveness of expression.

18. Transfer the use of the newly acquired vocal behaviors from the clinic to natural settings. (35)

35. Role-play different scenarios with the client (e.g., shopping or going to a restaurant), noting the instances when the client effectively uses his/her newly acquired vocal behaviors then accompany him/her on trip away from the clinic and record the extent to which the new voice is consistently used, continuing practice away from the clinic intermittently until his/her new voice is generalized.

___. _____   ___. _____
    _____   _____
___. _____   ___. _____
    _____   _____
___. _____   ___. _____
    _____   _____

DIAGNOSTIC SUGGESTIONS:

Axis I: 307.9   Communication Disorder NOS

Appendix A

ANNOTATED BIBLIOGRAPHY FOR PROFESSIONALS

Accent Reduction

Blackmer, E. R., and Ferrier, L. J. (1996). *Speech Works: The Accent Reduction Tool* (computer program). Campton, NH: Trinity Software. (Provides computer simulations of articulation placements for English sounds.)

Northern, J. L., and Downs, M. P. (2002). *Hearing in Children* (5th ed.). Philadelphia, PA: Lippincott, Williams, and Wilkins. (Describes audiological screening techniques and criteria).

Secord, W. (1981). *Eliciting Sounds: Techniques for Clinicians*. San Antonio, TX: Psychological Corporation. (Describes techniques for correcting articulatory placement for target phonemes).

Sikorski, L. D. (1988). *The Consonant Variations of American English*. Santa Ana, CA: LDS and Associates. (Provides techniques for learning English consonants.)

Sikorski, L. D. (1988). *The Vowel Variations of American English*. Santa Ana, CA: LDS and Associates. (Provides techniques for learning English vowels.)

Sikorski, L. D. (1989). *Proficiency in Oral English Communication: An Assessment Battery of Accented English*. Santa Ana, CA: LDS and Associates. (Provides a structured assessment of client's English speaking skills.)

Sikorski, L. D. (1993). *Mastering Effective English Communication Cassette Series*. Santa Ana, CA: LDS and Associates. (Provides audiocassettes to help the client practice English sounds.)

Stern, D. (1995). *Accent Reduction: Courses, Units, and Private Lessons*. Lyndonville, VT: Dialect Accent Specialists. (Provides training techniques to help the client reduce his/her accent.)

Wilner, L. K. (1993). *Medically Speaking: Accent Modification for the Medical Profession*. Santa Ana, CA: LDS Associates. (Provides specific phrases needed for the medical professions.)

Alaryngeal Speech

Andrews, M. (1999). *Manual of Voice Treatment*. San Diego, CA: Singular. (Provides descriptions of "Surgical Prosthetic Options" for voice restoration and the SLP's role in management of the tracheoesophageal prosthesis.)

Aphasia

Burns, M. S., and Halper, A. S. (1988). *Speech/Language Treatment of the Aphasias.*
Rockville, MD: Aspen Publishers, Inc. (See Exhibit 5-9 for self-cueing techniques in
the treatment of aphasias. See Exhibits 5-11 and 5-12 for questioning techniques
designed to elicit targeted grammatical constructs.)

Darley, F. L. (1984). *Aphasia.* Philadelphia, PA: Saunders. (Techniques are described to
help the client demonstrate comprehension of verbally presented material by asking
pertinent questions.)

Helm-Estabrook, N., Fitzpatrick, P., and Barresi, B. (1982). Visual Action Therapy for
Global Aphasia. *Journal of Speech and Hearing Disorders*, 47(4): 385–389. (Various
techniques associated with VAT are described to help the client increase focus and
awareness of visual stimuli.)

Helm-Estabrook, N. (1992). "Exploring the Right Hemisphere for Language
Rehabilitation: Melodic Intonation Therapy." In E. Perceman (Ed.), *Cognitive
Processing in the Right Hemisphere.* New York: Academic Press. (Describes melodic
intonation therapy techniques used to facilitate the client's verbal output.)

LaPointe, L. (1985). "Aphasia Therapy: Some Principles and Strategies for Treatment."
In D. F. Johns (Ed.), *Clinical Management of Neurogenic Communication Disorders.*
Boston, MA: Little, Brown and Company. (Describes techniques in which the client
combines familiar words into grammatical units. Also, techniques are described to
help the client demonstrate comprehension of verbally presented material through
the asking of pertinent questions.)

Apraxia

Helm-Estabrook, N., Fitzpatrick, P., and Barresi, B. (1982). "Visual Action Therapy for
Global Aphasia." *Journal of Speech and Hearing Disorders*, 47(4): 385–389.
(Various techniques associated with VAT are described to help the client increase
focus and awareness of visual stimuli.)

Rosenbeck, J. (1984). "Treating Apraxia of Speech." In D. Johns (Ed.), *Clinical
Management of Neurogenic Communication Disorders.* Boston, MA: Little, Brown
and Company. (Provides a general approach to the treatment of apraxia as well as
many useful facilitative and compensatory strategies for communication.)

Augmentative/Alternative Communication

Beukelman, D. R., Yorkston, K. M., and Dowden, P. A. (1985). *Communication
Augmentation: A Casebook of Clinical Management.* Austin, TX: Pro-Ed. (Describes
treatment approaches to specific cases.)

Cerebral Palsy

Miller, J. F. (1981). *Assessing Language Production in Children: Experimental Procedures*. Baltimore, MD: University Park Press. (Describes recording and analysis techniques for documenting the client's conversational skills.)

Robertson, S. J., and Thomson, F. (2001). *Working with Dysarthrics: A Practical Guide to Therapy for Dysarthria*. Oxon, UK: Speechmark. (Describes facial stimulation techniques used by parents to strengthen the client's facial muscles.)

Stamer, M. (2000). *Posture and Movement of the Child with Cerebral Palsy*. San Antonio, TX: Therapy Skill Builders. (Provides information useful to the client with cerebral palsy about the respiratory system and its role in speech production.)

Cleft Palate

Alberry, L., and Russell, J. (1994). *Cleft Palate Sourcebook*. Oxon, UK: Winslow. (Describe strategies for teaching parents to stimulate the client's lips, tongue, and alveolar ridge, as well as strategies to eliminate glottal stop and pharyngeal fricative substitution.)

Bleile, K. (1995). *Manual of Articulation and Phonological Disorders*. San Diego, CA: Singular. (Describes techniques used to analyze the client's use of speech skills.)

Bzoch, K. E. (1997). "Clinical Assessment, Evaluation, and Management of 11 Categorical Aspects of Cleft Palate Speech Disorders." In K. E. Bzoch (Ed.), *Communicative Disorders Related to Cleft Lip and Palate*. Austin, TX: Pro-Ed. (Describes the Communication Disorders Clinical Tests used to determine whether the client is using appropriate phonation.)

Bzoch, K. R. (1997). "Rationale, Methods, and Techniques of Cleft Palate Speech Therapy." In K. E. Bzoch (Ed.), *Communicative Disorders Related to Cleft Lip and Palate*. Austin, TX: Pro-Ed. (Describes techniques for using visual and tactile cues to encourage the oral airflow necessary for stops, fricatives, and affricates.)

D'Antonio, L. L., and Scherer, N. (1995). "The Evaluation of Speech Disorders Associated with Clefting" (pp. 176–220). In R. J. Schprintzen and J. Bardach (Eds.). *Cleft Palate Speech Management: A Multidisciplinary Approach*. St. Louis, MO: Mosby. (Describes techniques useful for evaluating physical structures necessary in speech production.)

Miller, J. F. (1981). *Assessing Language Production in Children: Experimental Procedures*. Baltimore, MD: University Park Press. (Describes recording and analysis techniques for documenting the client's conversational skills.)

Peterson-Falzone, S. J., Hardin-Jones, M. A., and Karnell, M. P. (2001). *Cleft Palate Speech* (3rd ed.). St. Louis, MO: Mosby. (Describes strategies to eliminate glottal stop and pharyngeal fricative substitution.)

Secord, W. (1981). *Eliciting Sounds: Techniques for Clinicians*. San Antonio, TX: Psychological Corporation. (Describes strategies for eliciting sounds to strengthen the production of affricates, fricatives, and plosives and to eliminate lateral lisping of the /s/ and /z/ sounds.)

Stengelhofen, J. (1990). *Working with Cleft Palate*. Oxon, UK: Winslow. (Strategies for teaching parents to stimulate the client's lips, tongue, and alveolar ridge. Also contains strategies to help reduce hyponasality of voice.)

Trost-Cardomone, J. E., and Bernthal, J. E. (1993). "Articulation Assessment Procedures and Treatment Decisions." In K. T. Moller and C. D. Starr (Eds.), *Cleft Palate Interdisciplinary Issues and Treatment for Clinicians by Clinicians*. Austin, TX: Pro-Ed. (Detailed procedures for evaluating the client's stimuability skills for error sounds.)

Developmental Apraxia of Speech

American Speech-Language-Hearing Association. (1997). *Guidelines for Audiologic Screening*. Rockville, MD: Author. (Describes audiological screening techniques and criteria.)

Crary, M. A. (1993). *Developmental Motor Speech Disorders*. San Diego, CA: Singular. (Describes specific techniques for evaluating oral-motor strengths and weaknesses. Also describes therapeutic approaches to use with developmental apraxia of speech.)

Hall, P. K., Jordan, L. S., and Robin, D. A. (1993). *Developmental Apraxia of Speech: Theory and Clinical Experience*. Austin, TX: Pro-Ed. (Describes techniques for writing different consonant-vowel combinations to increase the accuracy of consonant-vowel and vowel-consonant productions.)

Northern, J. L., and Downs, M. P. (2002). *Hearing in Children* (5th ed.). Philadelphia, PA: Lippincott, Williams, and Wilkins. (Describes audiological screening techniques and criteria.)

Secord, W. (1981). *Eliciting Sounds: Techniques for Clinicians*. San Antonio, TX: Psychological Corporation. (Describes techniques for correcting articulatory placement for target phonemes.)

Velleman, S. (2002). *Childhood Apraxia of Speech Resource Guide*. San Diego, CA: Singular. (Describes techniques for practicing consonant-vowel combinations that include increasingly difficult coarticulatory positions.)

Yorkston, K. M., Beukelman, D. R., Strand, E. A., and Bell, K. R. (1999). *Management of Motor Speech Disorders in Children and Adults* (2nd ed.). Austin, TX: Pro-Ed. (Describes therapeutic approaches to use with developmental apraxia of speech.)

Dysarthria

Fairbanks, G. (1960). *Voice and Articulation Drill-book* (2nd ed.). New York: Harper. (Describes contrastive drills used to train the client in speaking with appropriate stress and emphasis patterns.)

Rosenbeck, J., and LaPointe, L. (1984). The Dysarthrias: Description, Diagnosis, and Treatment. In D. Johns (Ed.), *Clinical Management of Neurogenic Communication Disorders*. Boston, MA: Little, Brown and Company. (Provides criteria for diagnosis of Dysarthria as well as treatment techniques.)

Dysphagia—Adult

Cherney, L. (Ed.) (1994). *Clinical Management of Dysphagia in Children and Adults*. Gaithersburg: Aspen. (In Chapter 3, there are descriptions of techniques for an oral-motor exam and a swallow evaluation.)

Logemann, J. (1998). *Evaluation and Treatment of Swallowing Disorders*. San Diego, CA: College Hill. (Describes strategies to help the client improve mastication and improve bolus control. Also provides information on thermal stimulation and improving the swallow reflex.)

Swigert, N. (1996). *The Source for Dysphagia*. East Moline, IL: LinguiSystems. (Provides a description of lip strengthening exercises and bolus propulsion techniques.)

Dysphagia—Child

Cherney, L. (Ed.). (1994). *Clinical Management of Dysphagia in Children and Adults*. Gaithersburg: Aspen. (In Chapter 3, there are descriptions of techniques for an oral-motor exam and a swallow evaluation.)

Logemann, J. (1998). *Evaluation and Treatment of Swallowing Disorders*. San Diego, CA: College Hill. (Describes strategies to help the client improve mastication and improve bolus control. Also provides information on thermal stimulation and improving the swallow reflex.)

Swigert, N. (1996). *The Source for Dysphagia*. East Moline, IL: LinguiSystems. (Provides a description of lip strengthening exercises and bolus propulsion techniques.)

Fluency Disorders

Ham, R. E. (1990). *Therapy of Stuttering*. Englewood Cliffs, NJ: Prentice Hall. (Provides details on assessing and evaluating fluency disorders. Also provides information on the use of rhythmic speech techniques to address stuttering problems.)

Ham, R. E. (1999). *Clinical Management of Stuttering in Older Children and Adults*. Gaithersburg: Aspen. (Describes the use of the bounce technique to help the client overcome stuttering patterns.)

Van Riper, C. (1972). *The Treatment of Stuttering*. Englewood Cliffs, NJ: Prentice Hall. (Provides a description of the techniques of preparatory sets, pullouts, and cancellations to be used in the treatment of stuttering.)

Hearing Impairment

Erber, N. (1982). *Auditory Training*. Washington, DC: Alexander Graham Bell Association for the Deaf. (Provides techniques to help the client discriminate between different spoken words.)

McCauley, R. J. (2001). *Assessment of Language Disorders in Children.* Mahwah, NJ: Lawrence Erlbaum. (Describes techniques used in the assessment and evaluation of hearing impaired clients.)

Owens, R. E. (1999). *Language Disorders: A Functional Approach to Assessment and Intervention.* Boston, MA: Allyn & Bacon. (Describes techniques used to train parents to reduce the frequency of their directives and control of topics. Also provides strategies for helping the client to ask for clarification when communication breaks down.)

Paul, R. (2001). *Language Disorders from Infancy through Adolescence: Assessment and Intervention.* St. Louis, MO: Mosby. (Provides strategies to train parents to expose the client to new vocabulary during daily activities.)

Stout, G., and Windle, J. (1992). *Developmental Approach to Successful Listening II.* Englewood, CO: Resource Print. (Describes techniques for helping the client differentiate between familiar environmental sounds.)

Infants at-Risk

Als, H. (1986). "A Syntactic Model of Neonatal Behavioral Organization: A Framework for the Assessment of Narrow-Behavioral Development in the Premature Infant and for Support of Infants and Parents in the Neonatal Intensive Care Environment." *Physical and Occupational Therapy and Pediatrics,* 6: 3–55. (Describes techniques to help parents learn to chart the child's behaviors that indicate readiness for communication.)

Girolametto, L. E., Greenburg, J., and Manolson, H. A. (1986). "Developing Dialogic Skills: The Hanen Early Language Parent Program." *Seminars in Speech and Language,* 7(4): 367–382. (Provides instructional techniques for parents to follow the client's lead during social activities and to respond contingently.)

MacDonald, J. D. (1994). *ECO II—The Eco Approach for Adults Communicating with Children: Responsiveness.* Columbus, OH: Ohio State University. (Describes techniques to help parents increase the client's frequency of imitating the gestures, actions, and vocalizations of others.)

Owens, R. E. (1999). *Language Disorders: A Functional Approach to Assessment and Intervention.* Boston, MA: Allyn & Bacon. (Provides strategies for parents while teaching the client to increase the length of utterances.)

Paul, R. (2001). *Language Disorders from Infancy through Adolescence: Assessment and Intervention.* St. Louis, MO: Mosby. (Describes procedures for specific criterion-referenced assessment techniques for infants.)

Rossetti, L. (1996). *Communication Intervention: Birth to Three.* San Diego, CA: Singular Publishing Group. (Describes procedures for specific criterion-referenced assessment techniques for infants. Also describes procedures that positively assist the client's communication development in infancy. Describes techniques to help parents learn to chart the child's behaviors that indicate readiness for communication. Provides techniques for training the parents in maintaining the client's level of arousal and eye contact during communicative interactions.)

Sparks, S. (1989). "Assessment and Intervention with At-Risk Clients and Toddlers: Guidelines for the Speech-Language Pathologist." *Topics in Language Disorders,*

10(1): 43–56. (Describes procedures that positively assist the client's communication development in infancy.)

Warren, S. F., and Yoder, P. J. (1998). "Facilitating the Transition from Preintentional to Intentional Communication." In A. M. Wetherby, S. F. Warren, and J. Reichle (Eds.), *Transitions in Prelinguistic Communication*. Baltimore, MD: Paul Brookes. (Describes strategies for changing the client's interactive play routine and modeling appropriate communication intentions at the prelinguistic level.)

Wetherby, A. M., and Prizant, B. (1993). "The Expression of Communication Intent: Assessment Guidelines." *Seminar in Speech and Language*, 10: 77–91. (Describes strategies for changing the client's interactive play routine and modeling appropriate communication intentions at the prelinguistic level.)

Language Disorders—Adolescents

American Speech-Language-Hearing Association. (1997). *Guidelines for Audiologic Screening*. Rockville, MD: Author. (Describes audiological screening techniques and criteria.)

Bowers, L., Huisingh, R., Johnson, P. F., LoGuidice, C., and Orman, J. (2000). *125 Vocabulary Builders*. East Moline, IL: LinguiSystems. (Provides strategies for teaching the client to expand vocabulary.)

Boyce, N. L., and Larson, V. L. (1983). *Adolescents' Communication: Development and Disorders*. Eau Claire, WI: Thinking Publications. (Provides techniques to teach the client how to identify main and supporting ideas in the classroom setting, as well as verbal and nonverbal cues that signal important information.)

Damico, J. S., Hamayan, E., Callisto, T., and Fredrich, E. A. (1992). *Multicultural Language Intervention: Addressing Cultural and Linguistic Diversity*. Buffalo, NY: EDUCOM Associates. (Provides information on narrative styles typically used by speakers from other cultures or ethnic groups.)

Ellis, D. B. (2000). *Becoming a Master Student: Tools, Techniques, Ideas, Illustrations, Examples, Methods, Procedures, Processes, Skills, Resources, and Suggestions for Success* (9th ed.). Boston, MA: Houghton Mifflin. (Provides techniques to teach the client to identify main and supporting ideas in the classroom setting, as well as verbal and nonverbal cues that signal important information.)

Hamersky, J. (1995). *Cartoon Cut-Ups: Teaching Figurative Language and Humor*. Eau Claire, WI: Thinking Publications. (Describes the use of cartoons to help the client understand the figurative meaning of humorous vocabulary.)

Hoskins, B. (1996). *Conversations: A Framework for Language Intervention*. Eau Claire, WI: Thinking Publications. (Describes techniques for training the client in generally applicable social skills such as greetings, introductions, and requests.)

Larson, V., and McKinley, N. (1995). *Language Disorders in Older Children*. Eau Claire, WI: Thinking Publications. (Describes videotaping and audiotaping techniques used to analyze the client's use of language skills.)

Nelson, N. W. (1998). *Childhood Language Disorders in Context: Infancy Through Adolescence* (2nd ed.). New York: Merrill. (Describes techniques for evaluating the client's social, academic, and vocational strengths and weaknesses.)

Northern, J. L., and Downs, M. P. (2002). *Hearing in Children* (5th ed.). Philadelphia, PA: Lippincott, Williams, and Wilkins. (Describes audiological screening techniques and criteria.)

Owens, R. E. (1999). *Language Disorders: A Functional Approach to Assessment and Intervention*. Boston, MA: Allyn & Bacon. (Provides strategies for helping the client ask for clarification when communication breaks down.)

Paul, R. (2001). *Language Disorders from Infancy through Adolescence: Assessment and Intervention*. St. Louis, MO: Mosby. (Describes procedures for specific criterion-referenced assessment techniques for adolescents. Also provides techniques to teach the client to look for root words and affixes in academic texts. Describes strategies to help the client comprehend information in written texts.)

Language Disorders—Children

American Speech-Language-Hearing Association. (1997). *Guidelines for Audiologic Screening*. Rockville, MD: Author. (Describes audiological screening techniques and criteria.)

Damico, J. S., Hamayan, E., Callisto, T., and Fredrich, E. A. (1992). *Multicultural Language Intervention: Addressing Cultural and Linguistic Diversity*. Buffalo, NY: EDUCOM Associates. (Provides information on narrative styles typically used by speakers from other cultures or ethnic groups.)

Miller, J. F. (1981). *Assessing Language Production in Children: Experimental Procedures*. Baltimore, MD: University Park Press. (Describes videotaping and audiotaping techniques used to analyze the client's use of language skills.)

Nelson, N. W. (1998). *Childhood Language Disorders in Context: Infancy Through Adolescence* (2nd ed.). New York: Merrill. (Describes techniques for evaluating the client's social, academic, and vocational strengths and weaknesses.)

Northern, J. L., and Downs, M. P. (2002). *Hearing in Children* (5th ed.). Philadelphia, PA: Lippincott, Williams, and Wilkins. (Describes audiological screening techniques and criteria.)

Owens, R. E. (1999). *Language Disorders: A Functional Approach to Assessment and Intervention*. Boston, MA: Allyn & Bacon. (Provides strategies for helping the client ask for clarification when communication breaks down. Also describes role play techniques for using the client's real-life events to train in the use of complex narratives in telling a story.)

Paul, R. (2001). *Language Disorders from Infancy through Adolescence: Assessment and Intervention*. St. Louis, MO: Mosby. (Describes procedures for specific criterion-referenced assessment techniques for children. Also provides techniques to teach the client to look for root words and affixes in academic texts. Describes strategies to help the client comprehend information in written texts. Provides strategies for teaching the client to expand vocabulary.)

Language Disorders—Preschoolers

American Speech-Language-Hearing Association. (1997). *Guidelines for Audiologic Screening*. Rockville, MD: Author. (Describes audiological screening techniques and criteria.)

Gamble, M. W., and Gamble, T. (1978). *Let's Play Games in Language Arts, Volume K*. Skokie, IL: National Textbook Company. (Describes verbal games that are useful in teaching the client to use more complex sentences with conjoined phrases.)

Miller, J. F. (1981). *Assessing Language Production in Children: Experimental Procedures*. Baltimore, MD: University Park Press. (Describes videotaping and audiotaping techniques used to analyze the client's use of language skills.)

Northern, J. L., and Downs, M. P. (2002). *Hearing in Children* (5th ed.). Philadelphia, PA: Lippincott, Williams, and Wilkins. (Describes audiological screening techniques and criteria.)

Owens, R. E. (1999). *Language Disorders: A Functional Approach to Assessment and Intervention*. Boston, MA: Allyn & Bacon. (Provides techniques for training the client in the use of verb tenses in utterances appropriate for developmental age. Provides strategies for teaching the client to ask questions of others about their feelings or actions. Provides strategies for helping the client to ask for clarification when communication breaks down. Also describes role play techniques for using the client's real-life events to train in the use of complex narratives in telling a story.)

Paul, R. (2001). *Language Disorders from Infancy through Adolescence: Assessment and Intervention*. St. Louis, MO: Mosby. (Describes procedures for specific criterion-referenced assessment techniques for preschoolers. Also describes therapeutic approaches used to meet preschoolers' language needs.)

Mental Impairment

American Speech-Language-Hearing Association. (1997). *Guidelines for Audiologic Screening*. Rockville, MD: Author. (Describes audiological screening techniques and criteria.)

Northern, J. L., and Downs, M. P. (2002). *Hearing in Children* (5th ed.). Philadelphia, PA: Lippincott, Williams, and Wilkins. (Describes audiological screening techniques and criteria.)

Owens, R. E. (1999). *Language Disorders: A Functional Approach to Assessment and Intervention*. Boston, MA: Allyn & Bacon. (Provides strategies for parents when teaching the client to increase the length of utterances.)

Paul, R. (2001). *Language Disorders from Infancy through Adolescence: Assessment and Intervention*. St. Louis, MO: Mosby. (Describes procedures for specific criterion-referenced assessment techniques for mentally impaired clients. Provides strategies for teaching the client to expand vocabulary.)

Warren, S. F., and Yoder, P. J. (1998). Facilitating the Transition from Preintentional to Intentional Communication. In A. M. Wetherby, S. F. Warren, and J. Reichle (Eds.), *Transitions in Prelinguistic Communication*. Baltimore, MD: Paul Brookes. (Describes strategies for changing the client's interactive play routine and modeling appropriate communication intentions at the prelinguistic level.)

Pervasive Developmental Disorder—Asperger's Syndrome

Gray, C. (1994) *Comic Strip Conversations.* Arlington, TX: Future Horizons. (Describes techniques for the use of comic strips to teach the client rules for maintaining conversations with others.)

Gray, C. (1995). "Teaching Children with Autism to 'Read' Social Situations." In K. A. Quill (Ed.), *Teaching Children with Autism: Strategies to Enhance Communication and Socialization* (pp. 219–242). New York: Delmar. (Describes techniques for using stories about social situations to teach social skills to autistic children.)

Gray, C. (2000). *The New Social Story Book.* Arlington, TX: Future Horizons. (Describes how to teach the autistic client appropriate social interactions using written social story scripts that outline expected types of social communication and can be enacted while being recorded.)

Greenspan, S. L., and Weider, S. (1997). *The Child with Special Needs: Encouraging Intellectual and Emotional Growth.* Reading, MA: Addison-Wesley. (Describes a floor-time therapeutic approach for the client.)

Hamersky, J. (1995). *Cartoon Cut-Ups: Teaching Figurative Language and Humor.* Eau Claire, WI: Thinking Publications. (Describes the use of cartoons to help the client understand the figurative meaning of humorous vocabulary.)

Janzen, J. (1996). *Understanding the Nature of Autism: A Practical Guide.* San Antonio TX: Therapy Skill Builders. (Provides a description of environmental supports that can be used to maximize autistic clients' communicative success.)

Mesibov, G. B. (1994). "A Comprehensive Program for Serving People with Autism and Their Families: The TEACCH Model." In J. L. Matson (Ed.), *Autism in Children with Adults: Etiology, Assessment, and Intervention* (pp. 85–97). Pacific Grove, CA: Brookes/Cole. (Provides a description of the TEACCH model for treating autistic children.)

Quill, K. A. (1995). "Enhancing Children's Social-Communicative Interactions." In K. A. Quill (Ed.), *Teaching Children with Autism: Strategies to Enhance Communication and Socialization* (pp. 163–190). New York: Delmar. (Provides descriptions of techniques to enhance inflections in the autistic client's speech patterns.)

Rinaldi, W. (1992). *The Social Use of Language Programme.* Windsor, ON: NFER-Fulton. (Provides a description of social-pragmatic approaches to treating autistic children.)

Snyder-McLean, L., McLean, J., Etta-Schoeder, R., and Rogers, N. (1984). "Structuring Joint Action Routines: A Strategy for Facilitating Communication in the Classroom." *Seminars in Speech and Language,* 5: 213–228. (Provides a description of how to structure joint social interactions using scripts of facial expressions, body language, phrases, and sentence structures.)

Spector, C. C. (1997). *Saying One Thing, Meaning Another.* Eau Claire: WI: Thinking Publications. (Describes the use of newspaper material to teach figurative language that includes multiple meanings and humorous references.)

Pervasive Developmental Disorder—Autism

Beukelman, D. R., and Mirenda, P. (1992). *Augmentative and Alternative Communication: Management of Severe Communication Disorders in Children and Adults*. Baltimore, MD: Paul Brookes. (Describes the use of augmentative or alternative communication to be used in communicating needs and desires.)

Fox, L., Dunlap, G., and Buschbacher, P. (2000). "Understanding and Intervening with Young Children's Problem Behaviors: A Comprehensive Approach." In A. M. Wetherby and B. M. Prizant (Eds.), *Communication and Language in Autism and Pervasive Developmental Disorder: A Developmental Perspective* (pp. 307–332). Baltimore, MD: Paul H. Brookes. (Describes strategies for overcoming challenging behaviors.)

Frost, L., and Bondy, A. (1996). *Picture Exchange Communication System*. Newark, NJ: Pyramid Educational Products. (Describes the use of pictures in communicating needs and desires.)

Gray, C. (2000). *The New Social Story Book*. Arlington, TX: Future Horizons. (Describes how to teach the autistic client appropriate social interactions using written social story scripts that outline expected types of social communication and can be enacted while being recorded.)

Greenspan, S. L., and Weider, S. (1998). *The Child with Special Needs: Encouraging Intellectual and Emotional Growth*. Reading, MA: Addison-Wesley. (Describes therapeutic approaches for the autistic client. Also describes floor-time intervention that uses natural adult-child interactions to facilitate social communication.)

Kientz, M. A. (1996). "Sensory Based Needs in Children with Autism: Motivation for Behavior and Suggestions for Intervention." *American Occupational Therapy Association Developmental Disabilities Special Interest Section Newsletter*, 19(3): 1–3. (Provides guidance for designing sensory integration interventions to reduce the client's hyperactivity or hypoactivity.)

Koegel, L. K. (1995). "Communication and Language Intervention." In R. L. Koegel and L. K. Koegel (Eds.), *Teaching Children with Autism: Strategies for Initiating Positive Interactions and Improving Learning Opportunities* (pp. 17–32). Baltimore, MD: Paul H. Brookes. (Describes techniques for prompting the client to use questions to initiate conversation.)

Mesibov, G. B. (1994). "A Comprehensive Program for Serving People with Autism and Their Families: The TEACCH Model." In J. L. Matson (Ed.), *Autism in Children with Adults: Etiology, Assessment, and Intervention* (pp. 85–97). Pacific Grove, CA: Brookes/Cole. (Provides a description of the TEACCH model for treating autistic children.)

Prizant, B. (1983). "Language Acquisition and Communicative Behavior in Autism: Word and Understanding of the 'Whole' of It." *Journal of Speech and Hearing Disorders*, 48: 296–307. (Explains the autistic client's use of immediate and delayed echolalia to communicate.)

Warren, S. F., and Yoder, P. J. (1998). Facilitating the Transition from Preintentional to Intentional Communication. In A. M. Wetherby, S. F. Warren, and J. Reichle (Eds.), *Transitions in Prelinguistic Communication*. Baltimore, MD: Paul Brookes. (Describes strategies for changing the client's interactive play routine and modeling appropriate communication intentions at the prelinguistic level.)

Phonological Disorders

American Speech-Language-Hearing Association. (1997). *Guidelines for Audiologic Screening.* Rockville, MD: Author. (Describes audiological screening techniques and criteria.)

Bernthal, J. E., and Bankson, N. W. (1998). *Articulation and Phonological Disorders* (4th ed.). Needham Heights, MA: Allyn & Bacon. (Describes options for general therapeutic approaches to treating phonological disorders.)

Hodson, B. W., and Paden, E. (1990). *Targeting Intelligible Speech: A Phonological Approach to Remediation,* (2nd Ed.). Austin, TX: Pro-Ed. (Describes a cycles intervention approach to target phonological processes to increase communication intelligibility.)

Krupa, L. (1999). *Read Aloud Minimal Contrast Stories with Activities.* Greenville, SC: SuperDuper Publications. (Describes reading activities that provide practice on minimal contrast paired words to increase the client's accuracy in pronouncing target phonemes.)

Northern, J. L., and Downs, M. P. (2002). *Hearing in Children* (5th ed.). Philadelphia, PA: Lippincott, Williams, and Wilkins. (Describes audiological screening techniques and criteria.)

Secord, W. (1981). *Eliciting Sounds: Techniques for Clinicians.* San Antonio, TX: Psychological Corporation. (Describes techniques for correcting articulatory placement for target phonemes.)

Smit, A. B. (2003). *Speech Sound Disorder Resource Guide for School-Age Children.* San Diego: Singular Publishing.

Van Riper, C. (1978). *Speech Correction: Principles and Methods* (6th ed.). Englewood Cliffs, NJ: Prentice Hall. (Describes traditional exercises for practicing target phonemes to increase accurate use in phrases and sentences).

Right Hemisphere Dysfunction

Brubaker, S. (1983). *Workbook for Reasoning Skills.* Detroit, MI: Wayne State University Press. (Provides exercises to teach the client abstract reasoning skills.)

Burns, M., Halper, A., and Mogil, S. (1985). *Clinical Management of Right Hemisphere Dysfunction.* Rockville: Aspen Systems. (See the chapter "Diagnosis of Communication Problems in Right Hemisphere Damage" for guidance in evaluating deficit areas involved in right hemisphere disturbance. Also describes strategies used to facilitate memory.)

Lazzari, A. (1996). *HELP for Memory.* East Moline, IL: LinguiSystems. (Describes strategies used to facilitate memory.)

Tracheostomy and Ventilator Dependence

Dikeman, K., and Kazandjian, M. (1995). *Communication and Swallowing Management of Tracheotomized and Ventilator Dependent Adults.* San Diego, CA: Singular. (Provides an in-depth discussion of ventilator types and requirements, tracheostomy tubes and adjustments, and sample practice protocols.)

Traumatic Brain Injury—Adult

American Speech-Language-Hearing Association. (1997). *Guidelines for Audiologic Screening*. Rockville, MD: Author. (Describes audiological screening techniques and criteria.)

Ylvisaker, M., (Ed.). (1998). *Traumatic Brain Injury Rehabilitation: Children and Adolescents* (2nd ed.). Boston, MA: Butterworth-Heineman. (Provides a description of informal assessment procedures involving observation of the client's communication in various situations and conducting collaborative hypothesis testing.)

Traumatic Brain Injury—Pediatric

American Speech-Language-Hearing Association. (1997). *Guidelines for Audiologic Screening*. Rockville, MD: Author. (Describes audiological screening techniques and criteria.)

Blosser, J. L., and DePompei, R. (2003). *Pediatric Traumatic Brain Injury: Proactive Intervention* (2nd ed.). Florence, KY: Thomson. (Provides a description of informal assessment procedures involving observation of the client's communication in various situations.)

Body, W. (2002). *Collection of Similes and Metaphors*. UK: Pearson Schools. (Provides a collection of similes and metaphors for teaching figurative language.)

Ellis, D. B. (2000). *Becoming a Master Student: Tools, Techniques, Ideas, Illustrations, Examples, Methods, Procedures, Processes, Skills, Resources, and Suggestions for Success* (9th ed.). Boston: Houghton Mifflin. (Describes strategies for learning academic material using structured note-taking techniques.)

Hotz, G., Helm-Estabrook, N., and Nelson, N. W. (2001) Development of the Pediatric Test of Brain Injury. *Journal of Head Trauma Rehabilitation,* 16(5): 426–440. (Describes a pediatric test for clients with brain injury.)

Jarski, R. (1997). *Shall I Compare Thee: A Witty Collection of Quotable Similes*. London: Prion Books. (Provides a collection of similes for teaching figurative language skills.)

Moreau, M. R. and Fidrych-Puzzo, H. (1998). *The Story Grammar Marker Kit*. East Hampton, MA: Discourse Skills Productions. (Provides methods for improving children's ability to tell stories.)

Northern, J. L., and Downs, M. P. (2002). *Hearing in Children* (5th ed.). Philadelphia, PA: Lippincott, Williams, and Wilkins. (Describes audiological screening techniques and criteria.)

Wood, A. (1990). *Quick as a Cricket*. UK: Child's Play International. (Picture book for young children that uses common similes.)

Ylvisaker, M. (Ed.). (1998). *Traumatic Brain Injury Rehabilitation: Children and Adolescents* (2nd ed.). Boston: Butterworth-Heineman. (Provides a description of informal assessment procedures involving observation of the client's communication in various situations and conducting collaborative hypothesis testing. Also describes videotaping techniques used to identify the client's appropriate and inappropriate social interaction.)

Voice Disorders

Aronson, A. (1990). *Clinical Voice Disorders*. New York: Thieme Medical. (Describes voice evaluation procedures including the analysis of phonation, pitch, resonance, and prosody and the interaction of these components.)

Boone, D., and McFarlane, S. (2000). *The Voice and Voice Therapy*. Nedham Heights: Charles E. Merrill. (Describes techniques used in functional phonation, such as the "yawn-sigh" method. Also, techniques are described that teach the client to improve laryngeal hypofunction using exercise while phonating.)

Cooper, M. (1996). *Change Your Voice: Change Your Life*. New York: Perennial Library. (Methods are described for helping the client locate his/her optimal pitch voice level.)

Fisher, H. B. (1975). *Improving Voice and Articulation*. New York: Houghton Mifflin. (Describes relaxation exercises useful in the reduction of laryngeal hypertension. Also describes techniques used in functional phonation such as the "yawn-sigh" method. Also, Chapter 3 describes methods useful for the reduction of hypernasality.)

Moncur, J., and Brackett, I. (1974). *Modifying Vocal Behavior*. New York: Harper & Row. (See Chapter 10 for descriptions of methods useful for the reduction of hypernasality. Also describes techniques that are useful in reducing throaty sounds and improving the resonant balance of the oral and pharyngeal cavities.)

Appendix B

BIBLIOTHERAPY REFERENCES

Accent Reduction

Hope, D. (1999). *American English Pronounciation: It's No Good Unless You Are Understood (Book 1)*. Atlanta, GA: Cold Wind Press.

Alaryngeal Speech

Laryngeal and Hypolaryngeal Cancer. American Cancer Society. Available at www.cancer.org.

Aphasia

Lyon, L. (1998). *Coping with Aphasia*. San Diego, CA: Singular Publishing Group.
Parr, S., Byng, S., and Gilpin, S. (1998). *Talking About Aphasia*. Buckingham: Open University Press.

Apraxia

Hoge, D., and Newsome, C. (2002). *The Source for Augmentative and Alternative Communicaiton*. East Moline, IL: LinguiSystems.
Lyon, L. (1998). *Coping with Aphasia*. San Diego, CA: Singular Publishing Group.
Sife, W. (1998). *After Stroke: Enhancing Quality of Life*. New York: Haworth Press.

Cerebral Palsy

Cera, R. M., Vulanich, N. N., and Brody, W. A. (1995). *Patients with Brain Injury* (2nd ed.). Austin, TX: Pro-Ed.
Geralis, E. (Ed.). (1998). *Children with Cerebral Palsy: A Parent's Guide*. Bethseda, MD: Woodbine House.

Robertson, S. J., and Thomson, F. (2001). *Working with Dysarthrics: A Practical Guide to Therapy for Dysarthria*. Oxon, UK: Speechmark.

Schoenbrodt, L. (2001). *Children with Traumatic Brain Injury: A Parent's* Guide. Bethseda, MD: Woodbine House.

Cleft Palate

Moller, K. T., Starr, C. D., and Johnson, S. A. (1990). *A Parent's Guide to Cleft Lip and Palate*. Minneapolis: University of Minnesota Press.

The American Cleft Palate Educational Foundation, 331 Salk Hall, University of Pittsburgh, Pittsburgh, PA 15261.

Developmental Apraxia of Speech

Velleman, S. (2002). *Childhood Apraxia of Speech Resource Guide*. San Diego, CA: Singular.

Dysarthria

Caplan, L., Dyken, M., and Easton, D. (1994). *Family Guide to Stroke Recovery*. New York: The American Heart Association.

Sife, W. (1998). *After Stroke: Enhancing the Quality of Life*. New York: Haworth Press.

Dysphagia—Adult

Caplan, L., Dyken, M., and Easton, D. (1994). *Family Guide to Stroke Recovery*. New York: The American Heart Association.

Sife, W. (1998). *After Stroke: Enhancing the Quality of Life*. New York: Haworth Press.

Dysphagia—Child

Dailey Hall, K. (2001). *Pediatric Dysphagia*. San Diego: Singular.

Fluency Disorders

If Your Child Stutters. (1981). Memphis, TN: The Speech Foundation of America.

Self Therapy for the Stutterer. (1982). Memphis, TN: The Speech Foundation of America.

Stuttering Words. (1980). Memphis, TN: The Speech Foundation of America.

Hearing Impairment

Dugan, M. (2003). *Living with Hearing Loss*. Washington, DC: Gallaudet Press.
Pope, A. (1997). *Hear*. New York: Dorling Kindersley.

Infants at-Risk

Family-Guided Activity-Based Intervention for Infants and Toddlers [Video]. Baltimore, MD: Brookes Publishing.
Manolson, A. (1998). *It Takes Two to Talk: A Parent's Guide to Helping Children Communicate*. Toronto, Canada: Hanen Early Learning Resources Center.
Weitzman, E. (1992). *Learning Language and Loving It*. Bisbee, AZ: Imaginart.

Language Disorders—Adolescents

Boyce, N. L., and Larson, V. L. (1983). *Adolescents' Communication: Development and Disorders*. Eau Claire, WI: Thinking Publications.
Mayo, P., and Waldo, P. (1986). *Communicate: An Educational Activity to Reinforce Social-Communication Skills During Adolescence*. Eau Claire, WI: Thinking Publications.

Language Disorders—Children

Hamaguchi, P. A. (1995). *Childhood Speech, Language, and Listening Problems: What Every Parent Should Know*. New York: Wiley.
Muir, N., McCaig, S., Gerylo, K., Gompf, M., Burke, T., and Lumsden, P. (2000). *Talk! Talk! Talk! Tools to Facilitate Language*. Eau Claire, WI: Thinking Publications.

Language Disorders—Preschoolers

Apel, K., and Masterson, J. (2001). *Beyond Baby Talk: From Sounds to Sentences, A Parent's Complete Guide to Language Development*. Roseville, CA: Prima Publishing.
Schwartz, S., and Heller Miller, J. E. (1988). *The Language of Toys: Teaching Communication Skills to Special-Needs Children*. Rockville, MD: Woodbine House.
Weitzman, E. (1992). *Learning Language and Loving It: A Guide to Promoting Children's Social and Language Development in Early Childhood Settings*. Toronto: The Hanen Program.

Mental Impairment

Baker, B. L., Brightman, A., and Blacher, J. (1997). *Steps to Independence: Teaching Everyday Skills to Children with Special Needs*. Baltimore, MD: Paul H. Brookes.

McGarrity, M. (1993). *A Guide to Mental Retardation: A Comprehensive Resource for Parents, Teachers, and Helpers Who Know, Love, and Care for People with Mental Retardation*. New York: Crossroad.

Pervasive Developmental Disorder—Asperger's Syndrome

Ozonoff, S., and Dawson, G. (2002). *A Parent's Guide to Asperger Syndrome and High-Functioning Autism*. New York: Guilford Press.

Stanton, M. (2000). *Learning to Live with High Functioning Autism*. Philadelphia: J. Kingsley Publishers.

Pervasive Developmental Disorder—Autism

Powers, M. D. (Ed.). (1989). *Children with Autism: A Parents' Guide*. Bethesda, MD: Woodbine House.

Sussman, F. (1999). *More Than Words: Helping Parents Promote Communication and Social Skills in Children with Autism Spectrum Disorder*. Toronto: The Hanen Centre.

Phonological Disorders

American Speech-Language-Hearing Association, 1801 Rockville Pike, Rockville, MD 20852. Available at www.asha.org.

Apel, K., and Masterson, J. J. (2001). *Beyond Baby Talk: A Parent's Complete Guide to Language Development*. Roseville, CA: Prima Publications.

Hamaguchi, P. (1995). *Childhood Speech, Language, and Listening Problems: What Every Parent Should Know*. New York: Wiley.

Martin, K. L. (1997). *Does My Child Have a Speech Problem?* Chicago, IL: Chicago Review Press.

McCarthy, J. M. (1990). *A Child's First Words* [Videorecording]. Santa Ana, CA: The Chapter.

Retherford, K. S. (1996). *Normal Communication Acquisition: An Animated Database of Behaviors* [CD-ROM]. Eau Claire, WI: Thinking Publications.

Schetz, K. F., and Cassell, S. K. (1994). *Talking Together: A Parent's Guide to the Development, Enrichment, and Problems of Speech and Language*. Blacksburg, VA: Pocahontas Press.

Right Hemisphere Dysfunction

Shirk, E. (1991). *After the Stroke*. Buffalo, NY: Prmetheus.
Weiner, F., Lee, M., and Bell, H. (1994). *Recovering at Home After a Stroke*. New York: The Body Press/Perigie Books.

Traumatic Brain Injury—Adult

Gronwall, D. M. A. (1998). *Head Injury: The Facts—A Guide for Families and Caregivers*. Oxford: Oxford University Press.
Winslade, W. (1998). *Confronting Traumatic Brain Injury*. New Haven, CT: Yale University Press.

Traumatic Brain Injury—Pediatric

Cera, R. M., Vulanich, N. N., and Brody, W. A. (1995). *Patients with Brain Injury* (2nd ed.). Austin, TX: Pro-Ed.
Schoenbrodt, L. (2001). *Children with Traumatic Brain Injury: A Parent's Guide*. Bethseda, MD: Woodbine House.

Voice Disorders

Boone, D. (1991). *Is Your Voice Telling On You?* San Diego, CA: Singular Publishing Group.
Cooper, M. (1984). *Change Your Voice: Change Your Life*. New York: Barnes and Noble.

Appendix C

INDEX OF *DSM-IV-TR* CODES ASSOCIATED WITH PRESENTING PROBLEMS

Aphasia   **784.3**
Aphasia
Right Hemisphere Dysfunction

Aphonia   **784.41**
Voice Disorders

Asperger's Disorder   **299.80**
Pervasive Developmental
Disorder—Asperger's
Syndrome
Pervasive Developmental
Disorder—Autism

Autistic Disorder   **299.00**
Pervasive Developmental
Disorder—Autism

Cognitive Disorder NOS   **294.9**
Right Hemisphere Dysfunction
Traumatic Brain Injury—Adult

**Communication Disorder
NOS**   **307.9**
Accent Reduction
Alaryngeal Speech
Aphasia
Apraxia
Cerebral Palsy
Cleft Palate
Developmental Apraxia
of Speech
Dysarthria
Fluency Disorders

Hearing Impairment
Infants at-Risk
Phonological Disorders
Right Hemisphere Dysfunction
Traumatic Brain Injury—Adult
Traumatic Brain Injury—Pediatric
Voice Disorders

Diagnosis Deferred   **799.9**
Augmentative/Alternative
Communication (AAC)
Cerebral Palsy
Cleft Palate
Dysphagia—Adult
Dysphagia—Child
Tracheostomy and Ventilator
Dependence

Dysarthria   **784.5**
Dysarthria

**Expressive Language
Disorder**   **315.31**
Aphasia
Apraxia
Developmental Apraxia of
Speech
Language Disorders—
Adolescents
Language Disorders—Children
Language Disorders—
Preschoolers
Right Hemisphere Dysfunction

Feeding Disorder of Infancy or Childhood   307.59
Infants At-Risk

Mental Retardation, Severity Unspecified   319
Mental Impairment

Mild Mental Retardation   317
Mental Impairment

Mixed Receptive-Expressive Language Disorder   315.32
Hearing Impairment
Language Disorders—
   Adolescents
Language Disorders—Children
Language Disorders—
   Preschoolers
Right Hemisphere Dysfunction
Traumatic Brain Injury—Adult
Traumatic Brain Injury—
   Pediatric

Moderate Mental Retardation   318.0
Mental Impairment

No Diagnosis or Condition   V71.09
Alaryngeal Speech
Augmentative/Alternative
   Communication (AAC)
Cerebral Palsy
Cleft Palate
Dysphagia—Adult
Dysphagia—Child
Tracheostomy and Ventilator
   Dependence

Other Change in Voice, Dysphonia, Hypernasality, Hyponasality   782.49
Voice Disorders

Pervasive Developmental Disorder NOS   299.80
Pervasive Developmental
   Disorder—Asperger's
   Syndrome
Pervasive Developmental
   Disorder—Autism

Phonological Disorder   315.39
Aphasia
Apraxia
Developmental Apraxia of
   Speech
Hearing Impairment
Phonological Disorders

Profound Mental Retardation   318.2
Mental Impairment

Severe Mental Retardation   318.1
Mental Impairment

Stuttering   307.0
Fluency Disorders

Symbolic Disturbance   784.60
Right Hemisphere Dysfunction

Voice Disturbance, Unspecified   784.40
Voice Disorders